Twenty Tales from the War Zone brings together the most powerful, shocking and also hilarious experiences of his career. It includes amazing stories from the many wars he has covered, from Northern Ireland to Iraq, from Kosovo to Kabul. Whether crossing the border into Afghanistan disguised as a woman or being kidnapped at gunpoint in the back streets of Belfast, Simpson paints a vivid picture of what being a journalist on the front line is all about. It's a rollercoaster ride that is sure to thrill anyone who dares to join it.

TWENTY TALES FROM THE WAR ZONE

THE BEST OF JOHN SIMPSON

John Simpson

SHORTLIST

First published in 2007 by
Macmillan
This Large Print edition published
2007 by BBC Audiobooks by
arrangement with
Macmillan Publishers Ltd

ISBN 978 1 405 62218 9

British Library Cataloguing in Publication Data available

Printed and bound in Great Britain by
Antony Rowe Ltd., Chippenham, Wiltshire

Contents

Preface   1
1. Trouble in Belfast   5
2. Angola   12
3. Terror in Tehran   21
4. No Change in Iran   31
5. Beirut   38
6. A Flight in Italy   45
7. The Cannibal   52
8. The Berlin Wall   60
9. Osama Bin Laden   67
10. Robbed in Prague   73
11. Bombs and Bullets   82
12. Spies   90
13. Colombia   98
14. Princess Diana   106
15. Meeting Colonel Gadhafi   114
16. Smuggled in Disguise   122
17. A Short Walk to Kabul   130
18. The Capture of Saddam   138
19. Disaster in Iraq   146
20. Nelson Mandela   159

Preface

John Simpson, who has been one of our best television journalists for forty years, was born in south London towards the end of the Second World War. He had rather a lonely childhood, being mostly brought up by his father in London and Suffolk after his parents separated. After school, he went to Cambridge University and from there to the BBC. He joined the BBC as a sub-editor in the Radio Newsroom in 1966 when he was only twenty-two. He soon became a political reporter and attracted his own publicity when Harold Wilson apparently punched him in the stomach after John had asked him if he was going to call an election. He became the BBC's Ireland correspondent, based in Dublin in the early 1970s, covering the

Troubles in Northern Ireland, but he then switched to foreign affairs. He was sent to Angola, a country in south-central Africa, where he covered the vicious civil war of the 1970s—an experience he has said was the most terrifying of his entire career. After that, John was the BBC's man in South Africa for a number of years, before becoming the BBC's main correspondent in Baghdad, the capital of Iraq, during the first Gulf War. Despite often being in great personal danger, John stayed in Baghdad throughout the war, even after the BBC ordered him to leave. He has since covered nearly all the major events in recent world history. He was in Berlin when Communism fell and was back in South Africa to see Nelson Mandela released from prison after serving a twenty-seven-year sentence. It is almost as if major events just can't happen unless he's there to report on them. This book looks at the exciting places he has visited, the strange people he has met and some of the dangerous times he has lived through.

1. Trouble in Belfast

I first went to Northern Ireland in March 1971, to report on the killing of three British soldiers near Belfast, its capital city, one night. I caught the plane from London early on the morning after the murders. When you are working for television, there will always be a man with a camera beside you. On this trip, though, I was working for radio and so I was alone. It was my first reporting assignment outside London, and I was feeling very nervous.

I drove towards the city, and passed the spot where the murders had taken place. I stopped the car and looked around. There was nothing to show what had happened only a few hours earlier. The soldiers had been lured into a bar by a couple of girls. The girls had then gone off to get an IRA killer, who waited for the soldiers in an alley outside the bar. Then he shot them all in the back of the neck.

It was the first time I had been close to something like this. I got back into my car and drove on. The road went round the edge of a mountain and then I saw Belfast. The city looked gloomy and poor in the grey morning light. Later, I came to love Belfast, but now I was too scared to feel anything for it. I was only twenty-six years old. I missed my cosy London home, my wife and our baby daughter.

I got to my hotel, and rang the BBC office in Belfast. They told me that there was to be a funeral that afternoon which I should cover. An IRA man had fired at a patrol of British soldiers, and they had shot him dead. I drove as close to the cemetery as I could, and followed the crowd of people heading for the big event. On my way I came across Derek, a reporter for the London

Sunday Times, whom I knew slightly. Meeting him at this moment may have saved my life.

It was to be a full IRA funeral. That meant that the IRA would fire their rifles into the air over the coffin. I stood as close to the grave as I could, together with a group of other journalists. It made me feel a little safer. In my pocket I had a small tape recorder, and I wanted to record the sound of the shots being fired. That was the big thing of the moment in radio, because it was so difficult to get genuine sound of the IRA firing their guns. But I kept my tape recorder out of sight until I was ready. I didn't have long to wait.

I didn't blend in with the crowd, because I was wearing a sports jacket and smart shoes. The problem wasn't just that I looked English. It was that I looked like an Army spy. I acted like one, too. I secretly took out my tape recorder when I saw the IRA men raise their rifles to fire in the air. And I got the recording. I felt really pleased with myself. My first day in Belfast, and I had got the sound of shots on tape. Finally the funeral came to an end, and the crowd moved away. The small group of British journalists wandered off.

A hand gripped my arm. A man with red hair and an angry face was standing over me.

'It's an Army spy,' he called out to a group of the nastiest people I had ever seen.

'No, I'm not,' I said, as bravely as I could. 'I'm a BBC reporter.'

'So show us your ID.'

I didn't have it with me. I have never been very good at carrying my ID papers—I suppose I don't like the idea that I should have to—and this has often got me into trouble. Now it looked as though it might cost me my life. While we were standing there, I could see a photographer from the *Daily Mirror* being stopped, just as I had been. A group of men dragged him over to the edge of the cemetery and beat him almost to death. I could hear his screams as the boots went in. Apparently the IRA thought he had taken the wrong kind of picture.

The angry man grabbed me.

'Give him one up the nostril,' he said, meaning they should shoot me then and there.

At that point I heard a very English voice close to us. It was Derek, the man from *The Sunday Times*.

'Ah, John, I wondered where you'd got to,' he said calmly. He had spotted what was happening to me, and risked all sorts of trouble to come and help me.

'This is Mr Simpson from the BBC,' he said to the man holding my arm. 'Has there been some misunderstanding?'

Derek was so firm and certain that the group opened up to let me past. I couldn't stop thanking him all the way to the main road. When I left him my hands were still shaking so much that I had trouble getting the key in the lock of my car. A group of IRA men followed me at a distance, to see what I did next. When I looked in the rear-view mirror as I drove off, I saw them writing down the car number.

That evening, back in my room at the hotel, I sat down on the bed. My hand was still shaking.

'It's no good,' I said out loud, 'I'm not cut out for this kind of work. I'm not tough enough for it.' I decided to fly back to London the next morning, and tell my boss that I wouldn't do any more reporting in Northern Ireland.

But then I ordered a steak from room service, and watched some television. And I remembered how I had taped the sounds of the IRA men firing their guns, which no one else had managed to get. Maybe, I thought, I should stay in Belfast for a bit longer before doing anything too hasty.

That night, though, I dreamed I was standing in an alley. A girl with red hair said, 'Give him one up the nostril.' I woke up shouting.

2. Angola

When the Portuguese left Angola in 1975, there was a civil war. Until then, this African country had been ruled by Portugal. Now, rival groups were fighting for control of the country. Two of these groups were known by their initials as the MPLA and the FNLA. The MPLA were backed by the Russians. The FNLA were funded by the Americans.

When the Russian-backed group looked like winning, MI6, the British secret service, got involved. They hired British ex-soldiers to go to fight for the American-backed group. I had heard that these men were going to fly to the neighbouring country of the Congo from Brussels, the capital of Belgium. I was based there at the time, and I went to talk to them.

At Brussels airport, they were easy to spot. They didn't like being interviewed, and were furiously angry with us. One of them shouted that if he saw me again he would kill me.

When they'd left, I wondered what would happen to them. I didn't have long to wait to find out. The BBC sent me to Kinshasa, the capital city of the Congo, to follow them the next day.

This is crazy, I thought on the plane. I was heading for the most savage place in Africa at that time. I tried to think of an easy way out, but there was none. And, anyway, I had never been to tropical Africa before.

After I'd checked in to my hotel, I took a taxi to the FNLA base. The driver looked scared when I told him where I wanted to go. The FNLA had been given total power to do what they wanted. When it looked as though they were losing the war, they started executing a lot of their own people. They did it at the base.

As soon as we got there, and I

13

walked over to the entrance, I heard shots from behind the wall. Then four men came out through the gate. One of them was a British hired soldier, or mercenary, who had been in the airport at Brussels the day before. He had said he wouldn't forget my face, and he was right. He shouted out and began to run towards me. I dodged through cars and burst through a crowd of nervous locals. My taxi driver was too scared to wait for me, but luckily I caught up with him just as he was starting to drive away. I don't know what made me do it, but as we passed the men who were chasing me, I stuck two fingers up at them.

I had a very difficult and dangerous time during the next couple of weeks. It turned out that several other leading mercenaries were staying at my hotel. They were violent and brutal. While I was sitting and talking to one of them at the bar, he stuck a lighted cigarette into someone's eye. Another took a particular dislike to me and explained in careful detail how he was going to kill me. Yet even paid soldiers behave conventionally when they have to. Shortly after threatening me, this same man went to the reception desk while I was standing there, and asked politely for his key. He walked over to the crowded lift with me, got in, and answered civilly when I rather cheekily wished him goodnight.

Every day I reported back to the BBC about the goings-on in the Angolan war, and about what was happening at this extraordinary, violent hotel.

One night, three more paid soldiers came into the bar. They were also British and they were experienced, too, but they were terrified. They explained that they had been tricked into coming to Angola, and how evil the FNLA were. One of them, Douglas, told me about another

FNLA man who was also a former British soldier. It was a story which would soon become known around the world.

According to Douglas, this man, Callan, was a devil. Whenever things went wrong he fell into wild, violent rages. Everyone was afraid of him. One evening, a young recruit on guard duty fired off his rifle by mistake. The next day, Callan called the whole guard of fourteen men on to parade. He called out the young recruit, shot him in the knee, then killed him with a bullet to the head. All the others were put into a truck and driven off. Outside the city, they were told to make a run for it. Callan and another man armed with a machine gun shot them dead as they tried to get away.

The three men in the bar with me had had enough of this dirty war. They were convinced that Callan would turn up at the hotel at any moment and kill them too.

'He can't do anything to you here,' I said, though I wasn't at all certain about that myself. 'I'll call the British embassy. They'll send you back to England.'

The next day, after getting them sorted out, I decided to leave too. I was much too frightened by what was going on to stay. (Afterwards, though, I realized I had made a serious mistake. It was an important lesson to me as a journalist. Never leave a story just because you're a bit scared.)

I was told to be very careful at the airport. Perhaps the FNLA would try to get me there, someone said. I had gone through passport control and was sitting in the filthy departure lounge when the trouble started.

Over the loudspeakers, someone called out my name and asked me to report to an airport official. I got up casually and wandered over to the men's toilet. It stank, but at least there were separate cubicles with doors. I went into one and sat down. Then I drew my feet up on to the filthy seat. While I waited, I put all my notes about Callan and the killings inside my shoes.

After a few minutes, the outer door of the toilets was kicked open. I heard footsteps. There were two men, perhaps three. They had shoes on rather than boots, so I knew they weren't from the army. I thought they must be FNLA officials. They walked halfway down the row of cubicles, then stopped. From the grunting sounds they made, I guessed that two of them were on their knees looking under the doors.

'Nothing,' said a voice. The outer door banged shut. Then the last call for my flight came over the loudspeaker. Would the men be waiting outside for me? I had no choice but to get on that plane. If I didn't, I would be as good as dead. I ran out, past a couple of surprised men in plain clothes, and handed my

18

boarding pass to the airline official. They couldn't get me now.

I only started breathing freely when we took off. Even then I thought that the two men sitting behind me looked familiar from the FNLA base. I was too terrified to be sensible.

When I got to Brussels I found out that another Western journalist in Kinshasa had beaten me to it with the story of the killings. I was very angry about that, because he had promised to wait until I reached Brussels. Still, it was a huge story and I spent all the next day broadcasting and being interviewed. As a result of my reporting, the BBC gave me a wonderful job as the correspondent in South Africa. And that changed my whole life.

As for Callan, who had murdered fifteen of his own men, he was captured in Angola. I went there to report on his trial. At the end of it, he was found guilty and sentenced to death. Throughout the trial, his face had been expressionless. But when the verdict was announced, he winced. Then his face just went blank again.

3. Terror in Tehran

The revolution in Iran happened because of a number of mistakes. Revolutions often start that way. Ayatollah Khomeini, the fierce, dark-bearded Iranian religious leader, had been in exile in the neighbouring country of Iraq for years, but in 1978 there were big demonstrations by his supporters in the streets of Tehran, Iran's capital city.

At this point the Shah (or king) of Iran, whose rule was becoming more and more unpopular, made his big mistake. He could have let Ayatollah Khomeini stay in Iraq, a virtual prisoner, cut off from the outside world, but, instead, he asked the leader of Iraq, Saddam Hussein, to throw him out of the country. Saddam agreed. So now, instead of being in a police state where no one could see him, he was free to go wherever he wanted. He chose to go to France. There, the whole world's press could interview him. From being quiet and hidden, he suddenly became the most famous person in the world.

I was one of the people who went to talk to Ayatollah Khomeini. He had taken over two houses on opposite sides of a street in a little village outside Paris. We filmed him walking across the street to the house where we were going to interview him. That was my first glimpse of him. His revolution was to be an important part of my work for many years.

We set up our lights in his sitting room. The Iranians had taken all the Western furniture out of the house, and everyone sat on the floor, on cushions and Persian carpets. The door opened and the Ayatollah came in. He was a small man, but he had a tremendous presence. He seemed to

22

fill the room. I wasn't sure what to do, so I said, 'Welcome,' and reached out my hand to him. I had forgotten that very religious Muslims do not like touching a non-Muslim. Looking down, he arranged the folds of his robe and pretended not to see my hand. It was done with such tact that I didn't feel offended.

Yet he showed no real interest in me. I was only the middleman for his message to the people of Iran. He told me he wanted to get rid of the Shah, whom he called a dictator. Then he would restore Islamic law, the Muslim rules of everyday life, to Iran. This interview was broadcast by BBC World Service radio as well as by television, and was heard by millions of people in Iran itself. Because of that, some people accused us of helping to start the revolution. Years later, I still got letters saying he must have paid me a lot of money—half a million dollars, some people said! But that was silly.

The whole world was interested in what Ayatollah Khomeini had to say, and anyway the revolution was well under way by that stage.

Not long after this, in November 1978, I went to Iran. Amazing things were taking place there. The sky was dark with the smoke from fires. People were attacking public buildings and setting up roadblocks all over the city. The situation was completely out of the Shah's control. Anyone who looked British or American was liable to be attacked and perhaps killed by the rioters.

I was in the centre of town with my camera crew, filming the start of yet another huge, angry demonstration. I realized I had to go back to my hotel to call London and arrange that night's satellite broadcast. We have a rule in my business that you don't leave your colleagues on their own when things get unpleasant—you stick with them. But the demonstration still seemed quite small and peaceful, so it seemed clear that I would have the time to go to the hotel, make the calls, and meet up with them a couple of hours later.

However everything took far longer than I had expected, and, by the time I had finished making the arrangements with London, the violence had really started. Great columns of black smoke hung over the area where I had left my colleagues. Our driver refused to take me there, saying that it was too dangerous. There was only one thing to do—I would have to walk. I felt horribly visible in my English tweed sports jacket, but I sang to myself to keep my spirits up as I strode along, and kept to the side roads where I could.

Whenever I came to a roadblock, I glared at the rioters like a lion-tamer. They looked at me and my jacket, yet they parted to let me through. It was a four-mile walk, but in the end I got to the place where I had last seen my crew. There were half a million people in the streets. How on earth would I be able to find two men in this crowd? Amazingly, I did. In the distance, above the crowd's heads, I spotted the film container on top of our camera. It was shaped like Mickey Mouse ears. I couldn't believe my luck. Still, when I reached them, they were so wrapped up in the drama that they didn't show any surprise at all that I had found them. They had got some great pictures, but the crowd was worked-up and very angry. We all knew that something bad could happen at any moment.

It did. A man shouted out that his brother had been killed by the army, but that the BBC hadn't reported it. He told the crowd that this proved the BBC was in the pay of the Shah. People who had been perfectly nice to us until that point suddenly became violent. They included a young man who had studied in Norwich. A minute or so earlier he had been telling me how much he loved England, but now he began punching us and spitting at us. That's what can happen when big crowds gather and get angry. People seem to lose all sense of proportion, and become savage very quickly.

Several people grabbed us, and I could see that it would end in our being pulled to pieces. It had happened to other people that day. Strong hands ripped at my jacket, and my arms were pinned to my sides. I could hear the cameraman and sound-recordist shouting, and I shouted too. The whole thing was now completely out of control, and it was obvious that we weren't going to survive this. A particularly nasty little man started beating me in the face with a broomstick. Fixed to the broomstick was a portrait of Ayatollah Khomeini, looking as grim as when I had seen him in Paris.

27

Blood from the blows was starting to run down my cheek. It made me really angry that this cowardly man would hit me when I couldn't defend myself. I roared with fury and somehow managed to get my arms free. Then I grabbed the broomstick out of his hands. All I could think of was hitting him back. I whacked him a couple of times, very satisfactorily, before I realized what an opportunity I had.

'I am for Khomeini!' I shouted, waving the broomstick in the air with his portrait tacked to it. Immediately our attackers stopped pulling us to pieces and became our best friends again. They wanted to carry us shoulder-high, but I quickly put a stop to that! Then they helped us to get through the crowd to peace and safety.

'Bit of luck,' I said as we walked away, trying to be modest. I expected the cameraman to thank me for rescuing him. But he was an old-fashioned BBC man, a good twenty years older than I was, and he believed that BBC people should always be absolutely neutral and unbiased, whatever happened. So do I. But I also think there are moments when you should be allowed to bend the rules a little, and this was one of them. He pulled me aside so the sound-recordist wouldn't hear.

'You know, John, you really shouldn't have said that about Khomeini,' he said, in an 'I've been in the BBC a lot longer than you' kind of way.

'But that's what saved our lives.'

'Well, I don't know about that, but it wasn't right, all the same.'

'But—'

He was already striding off down the road in search of more pictures. Looking back, I didn't feel very proud of myself. But I was glad to have got away with just a cut on my face and a few tears to my nice English tweed jacket.

29

I kept the picture of Khomeini, with the marks on it that look like rust but are actually my blood. It reminds me of how I escaped from what might have been a very nasty death. And of how I broke the BBC rules in doing it.

4. No Change in Iran

Tehran, the capital of Iran, could be both very scary and very strange all on the same day. At the start of the 1979 revolution against the Shah, the secret police and army would shoot at people who demonstrated in the streets outside the mosques. We drove around in the poor districts of south Tehran, looking for trouble. We soon found it. We happened to be driving past a mosque just as everyone came pouring out. The army and the secret police were already waiting for them, and got ready to shoot.

'Stop, stop,' I shouted to the driver.

'Are you sure we're allowed to film this?' asked the cameraman I was with.

He was very nervous, and unlike me he didn't like Iran at all. He thought the people were all a lot of dangerous lunatics. The cameraman doesn't come out of this story particularly well, but he was good at his job, and different things frighten different people. Four years later in Beirut, the capital of Lebanon, he stood his ground with great courage in the middle of an ammunition dump which was exploding all round us. He deserved an award for his footage then.

Now, though, he was much too hesitant. He got out of the car slowly, and took far too long getting ready to film. As a result he attracted the attention of the secret police. A senior officer ordered the soldiers to arrest us. They picked us up and threw us into the back of an army truck. It was very hot indeed.

'This is all your fault,' the cameraman said to me.

The sound-recordist said nothing. He wasn't looking well. We stayed shut up in the truck right through the midday heat, without any water. The sound man was starting to look really bad, and at times he seemed to be unconscious. The cameraman was groaning and rubbing his hands together, and blaming me for everything.

Eventually one of our guards went off to buy us some melons. After four hours of thirst they tasted wonderful. He told us, in Farsi, the language of Iran, to enjoy them because they would be our last meal on earth. I was the only one who could understand him, but I didn't feel I had to translate that to the cameraman. Then the guards let us wash our hands with water brought from a nearby mosque. They had said we could go and pray in the mosque before they shot us. I hoped they were joking, but I couldn't be sure. I didn't tell the cameraman this either.

There was a telephone box twenty yards away. I could see it through a gap in the canvas at the back of the truck. I pointed to it and told the soldiers I wanted to make a call. One of them stuck his rifle in my stomach.

I looked again at the state my colleagues were in. I decided that, come what may, I had to get out and ring the British embassy. I pushed the gun away from my stomach and climbed out. The soldiers didn't quite know what to do, but several of them pointed their rifles at my back as I walked towards the phone box.

In my life, absurd things often seem to happen. When I got to the phone box, I saw it wouldn't take the only coins I had in my pocket. I looked round. If I walked off to get change, I guessed the soldiers would shoot me. So I had to go back and ask the soldiers for help. Being Iranians, and therefore naturally generous, they gave me all the coins I needed to make the phone call, and more. They wouldn't accept any money from me in exchange. It was a present, they said. Then they pointed their guns at me again.

I got through to the man on duty at the British embassy. He sounded annoyed. I told him our problem, and eventually he agreed to do what he could. I came away feeling much better.

An hour or so later the soldiers' radio started to crackle. Someone shouted an order, and the truck's engine started up. We were driven to a secret police headquarters in south Tehran. We spent a long time sitting in the office of a man in plain clothes. He spent most of his time listening to someone on the other end of the phone line.

'*Bale*,' he would say, which just means 'Yes'. Then he would give us a fierce look. We must have been a pretty strange sight. The cameraman was rubbing his hands together and blaming me out loud for what was happening. The sound-man was still passing out now and again. And I was trying rather badly to do an impression of someone out of a 1950s British war film. I told the plain-clothes man that we were being treated terribly. I also said that, when I saw the Shah, I would complain about it all. None of it worked, of course. The plain-clothes man seemed to speak no English, and my Farsi wasn't good enough to threaten him properly.

Then came another phone call. '*Bale,*' he said again, but this time I felt it sounded different. He looked at me.

'Do you know Basingstoke?' he asked in perfect English. 'My wife comes from there.'

I started immediately praising Basingstoke and the famous beauty of its women, though in fact I had never been there. But I could see that everything had changed. A few minutes later a tray of tea was brought in for us. Then we were given one of the cars used by the secret police and taken to our hotel.

As we drove away, the sound-recordist sat up in the back of the car.

'Phew,' he said.

'Are you all right?' I asked.

'Course I am,' he said. 'I was just pretending, to fool them.'

The cameraman turned to me. 'I still think you put our lives in danger for no reason,' he said.

I didn't care. I looked out at the dusty streets of Tehran and felt great. Later on, I rang the embassy to thank the man who I thought had helped get us out of trouble. As I was doing so, he interrupted me.

'As a matter of fact I didn't do anything,' he said in his superior voice. 'We never do in these cases.'

5. Beirut

In 1982 Israel, the Jewish state, invaded Lebanon. This neighbouring country had been giving shelter to the Palestinians, who had been in conflict with Israel for decades. In July, I went there to report on it. I stayed in a big hotel in Tel Aviv, a seaside town in Israel, and every day we would drive up the coast to Beirut, the Lebanese capital, which was being bombed and shelled by the Israelis. As soon as I could get the BBC to agree, I went to stay in Beirut. It was much more frightening, but I was in the thick of it there, so I felt better. I settled in at the Commodore Hotel, which in those days was a small place where everyone quickly got to know you. A reporter friend of mine called Chris had been based there during the civil war that had started in 1975 and went on for more than fifteen years. He kept a parrot in the hotel. Its best trick was to whistle like an incoming bomb. People who hadn't heard it before would sometimes throw themselves in fear on to the floor of the bar.

Now the Israelis were besieging the city, and there were air raids every day in which hundreds of people died. The weapons that were used were terrible. I could imagine being ripped apart by a bomb when we were filming on the streets, or inhaling toxic gas and burning alive internally for hours before I finally died. These things were happening all round us.

One morning there was a very heavy raid by Israeli planes, and more bombs fell. We went to the main hospital in the part of the city controlled by the Palestinians. It stank. I'm sure I could smell it even before we got there. The operating theatres were lit with hurricane lamps because Beirut was without electricity. The victims lay bleeding on tables, while horrified, exhausted surgeons and nurses went about their savage business.

But the worst thing was the line of boys who had volunteered to wait outside the operating rooms. Each trolley bringing in a new patient would stop before going through the door. It was the boys' job to look for patients who had big pieces of shrapnel (sharp bits of metal) sticking out of them. Then they would pull them out with their bare hands. I have seen many terrible things in my life, but I never saw anything worse than this. Nor have I heard anything worse than the grunt the patients would give when the shrapnel was pulled out.

The Palestinians fought with courage, but soon a deal was struck for a ceasefire and for them to withdraw from Beirut. Their fighters would be taken off by ship and sent to other Arab countries. They would be allowed to keep their weapons.

The evening before this took place, I thought I would walk around the Palestinians' front line and get some photographs of the men there for my own interest. I didn't think I was taking too much of a risk. The ceasefire seemed to be working. It was a golden evening, and, at each position I came to, the men seemed to be enjoying themselves. They were pleased they had survived. They were also proud of the way they had fought.

I would climb up the banks of red earth which protected them. When I got to the top, they could all see me. Then I would say in a loud voice that I wanted to take their picture. The men would come out and pose for me in front of their weapons. They looked like pirates in their headbands. These were all foreign volunteers who had come to Lebanon to fight the Israelis. I found groups of Malaysians and Indonesians, and sometimes one or two Nigerians. It had been reported that there were three black Americans as well, but I couldn't find them.

The pictures were beautiful, and I thought I would offer them to one of the big news magazines. There had been only one difficult moment. A group of local Lebanese children had got hold of a rocket launcher, and they fired it up into the air over my head to frighten me. The rocket exploded in a spectacular way. But by now I was very used to bombs going off, and I didn't even flinch. That spoiled their fun. I wasn't even surprised that children should be firing rockets, which shows how violent things were in Beirut at the time.

I felt that I had done so well that it was worth taking a final risk. I came to one last position. The men here were Palestinians, and they were always more worried by journalists than the foreigners who fought for them. I called out, and raised my camera in the air to take a picture.

As soon as I did this, someone grabbed my arms from behind and tore my camera away from me. A gun was pushed against the side of my head.

'Spy, we will kill you now.'

'I work for the BBC. I'm not a spy, I'm a journalist. I'm taking photographs for myself,' I said.

'Spy,' he said again.

He pushed me forward, so that I could turn and look at him. He had a scarf round his head, and he looked crazy. His red eyes seemed to be crying. I couldn't quite tell whether this was from dust, or rage, or because he was so tired.

'Kneel down,' he said.

They made people kneel down just before they shot them. Oh well, I thought, at least it won't be gas or bombs that get me. I tried to pray and to think about my family, but it was hard to concentrate.

There was a click. I thought this was going to be my last moment alive. Then I heard the sound of the film being torn out of my camera, and the camera landed in the dust in front of me.

'Take it, spy,' said the man in the scarf.

It didn't seem to be a trick. I took it, and stood up.

'Go away and don't look round,' he said.

I did what he said. I was surprised by my lack of emotion. I wasn't even pleased or grateful to be alive. The days and nights of bombs and blood and fear had blunted my feelings, I suppose.

The next day the Palestinians left from Beirut harbour. They were waving and singing and chanting as their ships sailed out into the sea.

6. A Flight in Italy

I was returning from another difficult tour of duty in Beirut in 1985, and was going to take a week's break in Italy. My route took me to Milan, in northern Italy, where I boarded a flight for Rome, the capital. It was seven o'clock on a wintry evening, and already dark.

The plane was full. My seat was near the back, next to a quiet German man who was in his early forties. About the same age as me. He grunted. We both got our books out, and we both took a secret look at what the other was reading.

There was a pleasant buzz of chatter on the plane. Italians are sociable people, and like talking to complete strangers.

'The food will be very good, you know. It's only a short flight, you'll enjoy it. Can I get you a pillow? You look tired. Such a pretty jacket you have.' They were saying things like that.

The German man and I said nothing as the plane took off. People around us stood up, ignoring what the stewardess and the warning lights said. Long before the seat-belt sign was switched off, they were queuing for the toilet, laughing and smoking. In 1985 you could still smoke on planes, but not when you were standing up. They were all standing up.

The meal came round, and it was as good as the passenger across the aisle from me had said it would be. Then the trays were cleared, and our books came out again. My neighbour and I had still not spoken. Outside in the clear winter's night you could see the lights of little Italian towns below us.

We must have been about eighty miles from Rome when we hit the rain. It came down as hard as metal rods, straight across the windows. The plane tilted under the shock, and there were worried little noises all around us.

'That seemed rather strong. I'm not a good flier myself, I hope it won't get any worse. Don't worry, the pilot knows what he's doing,' they said.

The first bolt of lightning came a few seconds later. It didn't hit the plane, but it was so close that we were thrown off course. The screaming had barely stopped before another bolt struck the left wing and ran all along it, front and back. The bolt was as blue as a gas flame.

Italians are wonderful people, but it is probably better not to be with them when bad things are happening.

'My God, we're going to die! We're all going to die! God in heaven forgive me for everything I have done wrong. This is the last hour. Nothing worse can happen. O my mother!' they said.

Another bolt of lightning hit the left wing, and seemed to run along the body of the plane. Then another hit us on the right wing, and almost steadied us for a moment before we headed downwards.

The captain's voice came over the speakers. 'This is your captain. We are suffering some turbulence and some stormy weather, but I assure you there is no danger. This plane is very strong.'

His voice was drowned out by screaming. An old man rose from his seat and pulled open his seat belt, then ran down the plane towards the back.

The people round me were calling out, 'Death! Death! Father, I repent of my sins and seek forgiveness. Ah, my lovely wife, shall I ever see your pretty face again? Why did I come on this terrible flight, when Mario could have driven me?'

My neighbour and I sat side by side, fixed in a contest between

England and Germany to see who could stay calm the longest. He read his book, and I read mine. Neither of us turned a page. I don't suppose his eyes moved along the lines any more than mine did. I gritted my teeth and wished I could just be out of all this.

There was another bolt of lightning. Could the plane survive that, and the combined terror of two hundred Italians? I gripped my briefcase tighter. After going through all that in Beirut, I thought, I've let myself in for this.

'Jesus, Mary, Joseph and all the saints! Just let me live through this and I will do anything. Ah, my mother, look what has happened to your son! Forgive him,' the passengers were saying.

And then we were through it. The rain eased up. The storm faded. The man who had been kneeling down at the back near the toilet stood up and brushed the knees of his trousers. Someone laughed, and a couple of younger men shook hands. Everyone was smiling now.

The captain spoke again. 'So you see, ladies and gentlemen, this aircraft is very strong. There really was no need to worry. Now we will be landing in fifteen minutes, so please observe the no-smoking sign.' But everyone was puffing away in the happiness of the moment, and no one put their cigarette out.

The Italians were talking again. 'Now we have been through this terrible time together, we must see more of one another. I was never worried for myself, of course, but I thought you must be feeling so ill. I'm starting to feel hungry. It's strange how quickly an upset stomach can settle again. Would you like a cigarette?'

Beside me, the German man turned a page. I did the same, to show I really had been reading all along.

We landed soon afterwards. There

was a lot of clapping. Then we all stood up and reached for our bags. The Italians were all talking and laughing, like they do at the opera after it ends.

I looked at the German man, just as he started to look at me. I thought of saying, 'It was a no-score draw, then,' but changed my mind. I grinned at him instead, and he grinned back.

But we didn't say anything. We were the only ones on the entire plane who weren't talking.

7. The Cannibal

Over the years I have met plenty of kings, queens, presidents and prime ministers. But I have only met one emperor, and only one head of state who was accused of being a cannibal. And they were the same person.

It happened in 1986. I was in the BBC office in Paris talking to my friend Ginette, who ran it.

'So what's going on?' I asked.

'Well, we have the little emperor here,' she replied. 'Emperor Bokassa. From the Central African Empire. Now it's a republic again.'

I remembered him vaguely. 'Wasn't he supposed to have eaten the leader of the opposition?' I said.

Ginette pulled some articles out of a file and put them in front of me with her usual efficiency. There were dozens of items about Bokassa's career. He had gone from being a corporal in the army to captain, colonel, general, president and then emperor. There were stories about how he ordered hundreds of schoolchildren to be shot down in the streets, and about how he had been overthrown by French troops.

Many of the cuttings dealt with his trial. The star witness had been his French chef. He told the court that Bokassa had kept the opposition leader's body in a freezer. And, said the chef, whenever Bokassa felt depressed, he would order a slice off it! That had settled it: the entire world believed that the French had been entirely right to overthrow Bokassa.

Now he was in exile in France. I thought it would make a great story. The chance to meet a mad emperor cannibal doesn't come around too often.

'Don't forget,' said Mike, who was part of our crew, 'when he asks if you want a slice off the Sunday joint, just say no.'

We went to Bokassa's house. A short pudgy man in white with lots of gold hanging round his neck opened the door. He looked very sad. It was the Emperor himself. He led the way into the house, and, as I followed him, I saw something in the hallway that stopped me in my tracks. It was a very large freezer.

I pulled Mike back by the sleeve. 'Get him into one of the rooms and keep him there while I look inside the freezer,' I said.

I was quite scared. What if there really was someone in there? What would I do? The freezer was a chest model, with the lid on the top, a bit like a coffin. As soon as everyone was in the other room, I put my fingers under the lid and lifted. My arms were weak from nerves. Inside were a great many lamb chops, clearly bought as a job lot, and some packets of peas and carrots. No heads, ears, fingers or body parts. I leant down and reached in deeper. More peas and carrots, and some ice cream. That was all.

I walked into the room where everyone else had gone. I shook my head to let the others know I hadn't found any bodies in the freezer.

The Emperor was droning on about how he had been treated unfairly, and I took the chance to look around the room. It was full of evidence of his insanity. Plenty of deranged people have thought they were Napoleon, but only the Emperor Bokassa had actually put his fantasies into effect. Napoleon's face looked down at us everywhere from paintings and drawings.

There was a lot of gold paint all over the place. I suppose that made it look imperial, at least to Bokassa. This worried, sad little man in white, with his tasteless gold chains, hadn't just thought he was Napoleon, he had ordered hundreds of murders. And he had eaten human flesh as well. I was talking to a lunatic.

And yet, as our interview wore on, I became more and more caught up in his story. I even thought parts of it might be true, especially when he told me how badly the French treated him here. He said that he had indeed done many of the things he was accused of, and he was very sorry for them. It was true that he had ordered his army to shoot at schoolchildren, he said. The children had been demonstrating about expensive new uniforms they were told they had to wear.

'Weren't the uniforms made by a company which your own family owned?' I asked.

For people in the Central African Empire, that had been the last straw. It had brought people out on to the streets, especially the children. Ordering them to be shot had been a savage crime. To Bokassa, it was just a mistake.

'Your critics say you're crazy,'

I said.

For a moment his eyes went red, and I thought he might explode in a fit of temper, like he had in the old days. Once he beat up a foreign journalist (with his sceptre, I think) for not showing enough respect. But now things were different. He calmed down again.

'So what about the cannibalism?' I asked.

'Mr Simpson, I swear to you this was a complete lie. Never have I eaten human flesh. The very idea is revolting to me. I am not a wild animal. I did things which were bad, I know, but not this, I assure you. You must believe me.'

He stared at me with his crazy eyes. The strange thing was that I *did* believe him.

I checked out the story later. The chef had been the only witness to suggest that Bokassa had ordered him to cook slices of the corpse in the freezer. Bokassa, the chef had said, used to tell him which sauce he wanted. Then he would eat it with great enjoyment, the chef said. It was such a good story that it was just accepted at face value. No one checked to see if the chef was telling the truth. Who benefited? The French, because everyone thought they had been justified in overthrowing him.

After the interview my colleagues and I posed for photographs with the Emperor, and then we went into the kitchen to meet his wives. They were jolly, plump ladies, five in all, who all seemed very fond of the little man, cannibal or no cannibal.

We were the only journalists, French or foreign, who managed to interview him. The French police stopped everyone else from seeing him. Later he decided to return to what had once again become the Central African Republic. He wanted to try to clear his name, he said. He didn't succeed, of course.

He was jailed for life, and was said to howl at the moon from his cell. Then, since he was entirely harmless, the government released him. He died in poverty in a hut on the edge of the capital, Bangui, a few years later. He always insisted he was innocent.

When the news of his death came through, I wrote an article for a magazine about my visit to his house, and the contents of the freezer in his hallway. The title of the article was 'The Silence of the Lamb Chops'.

8. The Berlin Wall

On 9 November 1989, the wall between East Germany and West Germany at last came down. It had been put up in the early sixties to separate Russian-controlled East Germany from the free West. Suddenly people were told they could travel between the two parts of Germany without needing visas, which had been almost impossible to get before, and they no longer ran the risk of being shot. It was the signal for huge numbers of people to rush to the Berlin Wall and go through to the other side. The nights of 9 and 10 November were two of the most exciting in modern history. The entire Communist system, which had divided Germany for more than forty years, collapsed without a drop of blood being spilled. Soon the rest of Eastern Europe would follow. East

Germans could experience the simple joy of being free. The party continued all night, all day, and all night again. Even then it didn't stop.

At the moment the Wall came down I was in Warsaw, the capital of Poland, which then bordered East Germany It should have been easy enough to get to Berlin, which was only 320 miles away. But huge crowds fought to get on the planes to Berlin that evening. In the end I managed to get a seat on a flight which would get me there in time for our main evening news. Not for the first or last time in my life, I sat on a plane with a feeling of great relief.

I was picked up at the airport in Berlin and driven to the BBC studio, which was just a caravan in front of the Brandenburg Gate, at the centre of the dividing wall. Old-fashioned-looking Trabant cars, the symbols of this peaceful East German revolution, were everywhere, hooting their tinny horns, pumping out clouds of blue smoke, breaking down and being pushed. People crowded round them, shaking hands and kissing everyone inside. We nearly hit a car, but the driver just waved at us and grinned.

The road which led to the Gate was full of vehicles and people. It was a solid mass, and the breath of the people rose in clouds. The Gate was green in the lights. Only the day before, the land beyond it had been a hostile place. Now it was all the same Germany once again. It was one of the happiest nights I have been lucky enough to see.

The crowds were too dense to drive through, so we left our car by the side of the road and hurried on. I found that I had more time than I had thought, so I stopped and talked to everyone, getting a sense of what was happening. And it was then that I caught sight of the great miracle of my time. Hundreds of people were standing and dancing on the top of the Berlin Wall. They were waving sparklers, kissing, jumping up and down, singing. It took me some time to make out the words: 'We're going over, the Wall's gone!'

Then it was time for my live interview with John Humphrys, who was presenting the main news that night. I stood there with the shouting and singing and honking of horns in my ears. Someone put an earpiece in my ear so that I could hear John's voice.

'You look happy,' said the sound man. I was.

It was the biggest audience ever recorded at that stage for a British TV news bulletin. But it was a disaster, all the same. In the middle of an answer I was giving, someone from another network pulled the plug on us. They did this just in case they might want to use the line sometime later on. I fizzled out on the screen. In my ear I could hear

John saying the saddest words in live TV: 'Well, we seem to have lost John Simpson there, but . . .'

I felt very angry and small as I took off my microphone and wandered away.

However, it wasn't a night to be gloomy. Someone said we should all go for a walk along the Wall. It took us along a little dirt path through some woods. The woods had grown over the ruins of what used to be Hitler's HQ. After the city was split into two, this area turned into a wasteland. Wild animals lived there, like they do in the Forum in Rome. A few years before, I had been filming the site of Hitler's bunker on the other side of the Wall. A patrol of East German guards had come running up with their dogs, which trapped us, barking and drooling. Well, that sort of thing would never happen again here.

The little path was crowded with happy people. There was activity all along the Wall, and the constant sound of hammering. People were beating at the Wall with picks and chisels. The candles they brought shed a golden light on the Wall itself. The shadows of their picks were on the bushes, and on the faces of other people, and on the Wall itself. This was a very sweet revenge indeed for the decades of brutality and separation. They worked away at the joins between the slabs of concrete, making little holes which were slowly getting bigger. Sometimes you could see through to the no-man's-land beyond.

And there was a strange echo, which turned out not to be an echo at all. When the men with the picks stopped hitting the Wall on our side, you could still hear the sounds coming from somewhere else. There was a sudden outbreak of shouting and cheering. We realized that people were trying to break through from the Eastern side as well. At last,

65

a tiny hole appeared, and then grew bigger and bigger. In the light from the candles we saw a hand come through the little gap. The hand waved. A man on our side grabbed it and shook it. In all my life I had never thought anything like this might one day be possible.

9. Osama Bin Laden

I first set eyes on Afghanistan, the country between Iran and Pakistan, in January 1980, when the Soviet Russian army invaded. I was back there in February 1989, when the Russians left. Then in July 1989 I returned to make a film about the resistance groups there. We crossed the border, high in the mountains. Our aim was to go to the area where local groups from the hills were fighting with the nearby town.

Eventually we heard the sound of rockets being fired. We headed on, and found a group of fighters in a field next to the road. They were firing at the town, but they had little interest in what they were hitting. It could have been the army HQ or it could have been the local hospital. As long as it was somewhere in the town, they didn't care.

They were quite pleasant to us. At that stage moderate groups were still fighting side by side with more extreme ones. You couldn't tell the difference between them, because they all wore turbans and had the same guns, Russian AK-47 rifles.

For a while we filmed them firing off their mortar rounds. They cheered every time a cloud of grey smoke went up over their latest hit. I got ready to do my piece to camera while the firing went on behind me.

It was then that the figure in white appeared. He was clearly an Arab. His robes were spotless, and his beard was amazing. He looked as though he was in his late twenties, though it was hard to be sure. His AK-47 hung over one shoulder, and he had a big knife stuck in his belt. His boots must have been expensive. I had a good view of them, because he jumped up on a wall beside me and started yelling to the other fighters. He was pointing to us and getting excited.

'There is a problem,' said our translator. 'He wants them to kill you.'

There were four of us, and about eighteen of them, so I was relieved to see the fighters weren't very interested in what the man in the white robes was saying to them. In the end they had a show of hands, and voted not to kill us. It was a good job we had chosen this field to stop at. Later we found another one up the road where the more extreme fighters were in the majority. A vote there might have turned out differently.

The man in white couldn't kill us himself, because we were now their guests and they wanted to protect us for as long as we stayed with them. If he had attacked us, they would have been forced to kill him. Very comforting!

After the vote, we went back to filming my piece to camera. I had to kneel down so the cameraman could get a shot of the mortars firing as I spoke. Because of the ache in my knees and the loud explosions, I didn't see where the man in white had gone. After a while, though, I heard him again. Now he was yelling at a truck driver.

'He is telling the driver to come and run you over,' said our translator. 'He says he will give him five hundred dollars to do it.'

It wasn't much money, and I felt slightly annoyed that I wasn't worth more. It certainly wasn't enough for the driver, who shook his head and drove off.

The man in white ran off towards one of the arches under the road where the fighters slept. We followed him to see what he was doing. He lay on a camp bed, crying and punching the pillow. He was furious because he couldn't kill us. I almost felt like comforting him.

We left soon after that, but I never

forgot his eyes, or his beard. Even though he had wanted to have us killed, I still thought he looked splendid.

Nine years later I saw the face of the man in white again. The newspapers in America were full of stories about a rich Arab from Saudi Arabia, who had just become America's public enemy number one. He was Osama bin Laden, the leader of the Islamic militant organization al-Qaeda and the man who later planned the attacks on America on September 11th. There was his picture in the paper. It was him all right. His beard was a lot greyer than when he had tried to persuade the fighters to kill us, but his eyes still had that crazy, handsome glitter. He was a mixture of the Desert Warrior and Hannibal Lecter.

Not long afterwards I sent him a message through people I knew in Pakistan, asking for an interview with him. I got the answer a week later.

He told me that the Taliban, who were now in control of most of Afghanistan, did not want him to speak in public. However, he said, if he was going to speak to anyone from the media in the West, I would be the first. He wanted to speak to the BBC most of all, because the BBC was heard all over the world.

Times change, and we change with them. Osama bin Laden had once cried because he couldn't kill me. Now he wanted to talk to me in order to show the world that he was still a fanatic.

I didn't get the interview, all the same.

10. Robbed in Prague

I have only once in my life been robbed by experts. Of course, I've had plenty of things taken off me by petty thieves. Sometimes I have been forced to hand over money and small items at gunpoint. But this time it was different. This time it was a gang of trained crooks.

It happened in Prague, the capital of the old Czechoslovakia, a few days after what everyone now calls the Velvet Revolution of 1989, when the Communists were overthrown without a drop of blood being shed. Six years earlier, in 1983, I had made a film there about the way the secret police treated political and religious dissidents, those people who disagreed openly with the government. After that, not surprisingly, I was banned from the country.

When I flew in this time, without a proper visa, I gambled on the fact that the revolution was just starting, and I hoped the government officials I encountered would realize that things were about to change. At Prague airport the man behind the immigration desk looked at me and my passport very long and carefully. Then he examined a message which had come up on his computer. Presumably it told him I was an enemy of the state. In the end he made up his mind to ignore it. He stamped my passport, and gave me a little wintry smile. I was back.

The next few days were wonderful. I had a ringside seat, from which I could watch the end of the whole unpleasant, rotten police state which the Russians had created in Czechoslovakia. Still, it took some time to introduce a new system, and many of the old laws still applied. For instance, changing foreign money into the local currency, called crowns, still had to be done in the long-winded, expensive way of the past. I was short of time, because reporting the revolution and its aftermath took up twenty hours of each day. So I decided to change my money with a tout on the street. That was still illegal, but everyone knew the law would soon be changed. I decided to take the risk.

I wandered down into the Old Town. Today Prague is full of tourists, but in November 1989 scarcely any Westerners were there—except, of course, for journalists like me. There were few street lights, and the pavements were bad. The shops had old-fashioned things in them. The people were shabby and, in spite of the new hope that was dawning, their faces were gloomy and worried. I loved it, all the same. If I wanted smart shops and expensive Western goods, I could go to France or Germany.

The old part of the city was

beginning to empty of people. Today this is the part that stays open until past midnight, but in those days the streets were quiet by seven-thirty. Most of the shops had closed. The bells of the magical clock in the Old Town square were chiming. It was getting late to find anyone to change money. I walked up and down in my expensive coat, looking exactly like what I was—a Westerner looking for a deal.

It worked. A man came out of an old house and walked beside me. He spoke quietly and looked straight ahead.

'You want to change money?' he said in good English.

I said I did.

'How much?'

Two hundred dollars, I told him. That was a lot of money in Prague.

'Hmm. It'll take me a couple of minutes to get the crowns.'

I walked up and down a little more. By this time there was hardly anyone else on the street. I saw him again at the door of the old house that he had come out of. It was only then that I realized the house was being repaired. Workmen were still hammering away in one of the rooms on the ground floor and upstairs.

'I'm working on the house here,' the man whispered. 'Come into the hall. It's safer.'

I stepped into the hall. It was dark, but the light from the room with the workmen in it was enough for us to see to change money.

'So, two hundred dollars, that's 140,000 crowns,' the man said.

I showed him my two bills of a hundred dollars each. He looked at them carefully, then handed them back to me and began counting out the Czech notes.

At that instant there was an explosion of rage, and a stocky man came charging down the stairs.

'Christ!' shouted the man who was counting out the money. 'It's my foreman! He's a real Communist. Quick, give me the dollars. Here's your cash.'

He shoved a thick wad of notes into my hand.

'Run for it! He'll call the cops!'

I ran for it. What if the authorities caught me? Even now, when Communism was collapsing, I could be in trouble. It would be embarrassing for me, and for the BBC.

And yet, even while I was running, something was working away inside my head. How come, if it was so dangerous to be doing a deal with a Westerner, the man had shouted out a warning to me in English? That, surely, would be proof to the foreman that he was up to no good.

I slowed down. No policemen were running through the streets in search of me. I stopped in an alley and pulled the wad of money out of my pocket. There were a couple of one-hundred-crown notes on the top. But the rest seemed less familiar. I had a hollow feeling in my stomach as I looked at them. These notes were all Polish. There was huge inflation in Poland at that time, and the whole thick wad of money I held in my hand was worth about five dollars. If, that is, you could find anyone who would accept them. I had been well and truly robbed.

I turned round and ran back. In the old house the workmen were just packing up, and I spoke to one of them. Yes, there had been a couple of men hanging around. They were probably up to no good, he said. One of the men had gone upstairs, though neither of them was supposed to be there. They weren't working on the house, or anything like that. They just came in off the street. He'd heard one of the men shouting. Had they stolen something from me?

'No, not at all,' I said, 'nothing like that. No, I'd just been asking the way.'

'Oh, asking the way,' said the workman with a little grin. 'I hope he told you. So why did you come back?'

I didn't say anything and walked off. At first I was angry. Two hundred dollars was quite a lot of money to have lost. I felt such an idiot.

As I walked, the spires of the old city shone in the damp evening air. Everything seemed so beautiful. Now this country that I loved so much was free, and I had had the privilege of watching it happen. That was worth vastly more than two hundred dollars.

And then I thought about the details of the way the crooks had robbed me. How brilliant their timing had been! How real the money-changer's fear had seemed, how clever the Communist foreman had been! And, finally, how skilful the money-changer had been, hiding the genuine notes and pulling out the Polish ones from nowhere like a great magician. I had been given a masterclass in conmanship. It was an expensive lesson, but a show like that deserved a reward.

I laughed out loud. People on the other side of the square looked over to see who was making that strange noise in a silent city.

11. Bombs and Bullets

On 2 August 1990, I was on holiday in France. I heard on the radio that Saddam Hussein, the leader of Iraq and one of the world's most feared dictators, had invaded Kuwait, the neighbouring country. As a senior BBC journalist, that was the end of my holiday. Within three hours I was in London, and that was the last day off I had in six months.

Two weeks later, I was part of the first TV group to be let into Iraq. I stayed in Baghdad, the capital city, almost the whole time until the First Gulf War began, five months later. When it came, it was short and very violent.

It started in the early hours of 17 January 1991. Saddam had said that there would be two huge waves of bombing. Just before the bombs began to fall, four members of my team decided to leave. The only ones who stayed were Eamonn, a producer, and a radio reporter called Bob. A cameraman called Anthony, who had been working for someone else, offered to join us.

We decided to drive out into the streets to film the start of the bombing. It was 2.32 a.m. We ran out of the hotel to our car. 'Drive!' we shouted at the driver. But drive where? We hadn't had time to work it out. We were still shouting when guns and missiles started blasting all around us.

We took a fast turn into an underpass. As we came out of the other side, anti-aircraft guns started to go off beside us. Anthony yelled that he was getting it all on camera, but the driver was so scared he drove back to the hotel. We tried to set up the camera in front of the hotel. Then we heard the first sounds of aircraft. We're in for it now, I thought. The bombs and missiles that were going to be dropped on Baghdad had never been tried out in a war before.

Some secret policemen pulled us into the hotel. Inside it was dark and people were screaming. I lost touch with the others. Then I was forced at gunpoint down narrow stairs to a shelter. You could hear the first bombs falling around our hotel. The whole building shook.

I found Anthony and we fought our way out. We couldn't stand it down there. A guard tried to stop us, but we pushed past him. We ran up the stairs to the BBC office on the fifth floor. Someone was chasing us.

In the office, I crouched by a window and did a piece to camera. The man who had followed us must have heard my voice, and he started banging on the door. I thought I should get out, so he would follow me and the others could carry on with their work. I ran out, charging towards him. Further down the corridor I dodged into an empty bedroom and lay down. It was 5.45 a.m. A 2,000-pound bomb exploded nearby, but I fell asleep seconds later.

I woke up three hours later. Anthony and I found a driver outside who took us into the city centre. It was empty, quiet and very strange. We were chased by a car from the secret police, but managed to escape. Back at the hotel, I met up with the four people from our crew who had decided to leave. They were still waiting to be led out of Baghdad. One of them was standing by the window, and called out in surprise. He had seen a huge missile flying along the line of the road, at a height of about fifty feet. Some time later I saw one myself. It turned left at the traffic lights and hit the ministry of defence.

The four BBC people left. They even took the two flak jackets which were the only ones we had. They thought they might have to pay for them if they weren't returned to London!

On the second night, the US news channel CNN told us that the Americans planned to hit our hotel. Luckily for us, this didn't happen. Even so, we felt that we would rather die in our beds than be in that awful shelter in the basement. I had lost any great interest in surviving. I just wanted to see as much as I could of the war and report it. Since there was nothing I could do, I might as well enjoy myself. I opened a tin of oysters and had a large glass of whisky. Each morning, when I woke up, I was surprised to find I was still alive.

There was no electricity, water or food in the hotel now. The bathrooms stank. Day and night the raids went on, but we had become less afraid of them. Whenever the raids started, the security men would run inside, while we ran out to set up our satellite phone and start broadcasting. We would pass them on the way, but they were usually too scared of the bombing to stop us. Once, one of them turned and started shouting at me to get inside.

'There's nothing to worry about,' I said.

At that moment there was a sound in the air and a large bullet landed beside me on the steps.

'You don't think that's something to worry about?' he said. He picked it up. It was still hot, and he burned his fingers.

That afternoon the Iraqi government told us we had to get out of the country. Before we could leave, a cruise missile landed in the grounds of our hotel. I happened to be recording a piece to camera with my back to the window when it hit. There was a huge explosion outside. Everyone else in the room looked at me with strange expressions.

'It was a cruise missile,' one of

them said. 'It went right behind you as you were talking.'

Anthony and I went charging down to film the damage, but four guards jumped on us, and, although we fought hard, they took the tape out of the camera. The pictures on it showed the missile passing behind my head. I felt as if I had been robbed of a video of the Loch Ness Monster.

On the long drive to Jordan, as we were being thrown out of Iraq, I was very gloomy. I had been told (wrongly, as it turned out) that none of our pictures had got to Jordan. I thought I had done really badly on the most important story I had ever covered. When we got to the hotel, photographers began to take my picture and a large group of journalists were waiting to greet me.

It turned out that we had done rather well. The BBC crew who had left Baghdad had smuggled our tapes out. My broadcasts had been seen by huge audiences. After twenty-five years of work, it seemed that I had finally made it. But it taught me how unimportant and unreliable fame is.

12. Spies

The most exciting word in English is 'secret'. If you put it on the front of a newspaper or a magazine, people will buy it. It has almost the same effect that cover-pictures of Princess Diana once had.

Some years ago I found myself in the HQ of the Secret Intelligence Service, SIS. Some people call it MI6, but SIS is the proper name. I was having lunch with its boss, Sir Colin McColl. He was a charming man, with white hair and bushy eyebrows. Ian Fleming, who wrote the James Bond books, would have called him 'M', but he was really known as 'C'. This is the title all heads of SIS are given. It comes from the surname of its first boss, Sir Mansfield Cumming.

Sir Colin was the first SIS boss to be named publicly. It wasn't the first time I had met him. He had invited me to lunch once before, shortly after the end of the First Gulf War. I had just come back after almost six months in Baghdad, but it was clear to me then that Sir Colin knew a lot more about Iraq than I did.

That was in 1991. Now it was 1994. John Major was prime minister, and he wanted SIS to open up a little more. The Soviet Union had collapsed, the Berlin Wall had come down and there seemed less need for secrecy. So SIS invited some people from the media to come to its headquarters for a chat. I was one of them.

We had lunch in a grand room looking out over the Thames. I had already explained to Sir Colin that it was bad for a journalist to get too close to SIS. People might think you were on their payroll, working for them in secret. I wanted to be able to write freely about them, though of course I understood the need to protect their security.

Journalists and spies have one thing in common. They both deal in information, but the way they go about their jobs is entirely different. The spies need to keep everything to themselves. Journalists have a duty to tell everyone what is going on. In fact, I told the SIS people I would be writing about the lunch we were having. Someone coughed and had to drink a glass of water, but otherwise I thought they took it rather well.

Then I asked Sir Colin if he didn't find the idea that all spies are like James Bond rather irritating. To my surprise, he didn't.

'In fact, we find it rather useful in getting people to work here,' said Sir Colin. 'People link us to that image, you see.'

'British people?' I asked.

'And others. Other people more than British people, I should say.'

The British secret services have

always done well out of the legends that grow up around them. After the end of Communism in Russia, a general in the KGB, the Soviet secret service, told me that his organization had studied Ian Fleming's James Bond books carefully. Their library had copies of all of them. They read them to try and find clues to the way SIS worked. They didn't realize that Fleming knew next to nothing about SIS, and had only spent a short time in a different branch of intelligence during the Second World War.

SIS has a great sense of style. It likes to maintain an image of being clever and different from the rest of us, even today. I was told with some pride that one of the top people in SIS was a world expert on a type of oriental art. Another had been named as one of Britain's best novelists.

The old-fashioned idea of the man of action still played a part in SIS too. James Bond isn't dead. Once, in a cave near Kabul in Afganistan, some Afghan rebels told me how an SIS officer had made his way, through the snow, across land held by the Russians. His job was to bring money to the Afghan resistance who were fighting the Soviet army. The SIS officer was carrying a huge amount of money in gold, taped all around his body.

Although I had been invited to SIS headquarters by 'C', I had my own reasons for going there. I wanted to persuade him to let us make a film for the BBC on the way SIS worked. Despite the supposed new openness, 'C' didn't think this was a good idea.

'Our service is based on trust and secrecy,' he said to me. 'Our people place their careers and lives in our hands. I can't be seen on TV showing you round this place.'

This wasn't at all what I wanted to hear, of course. But Sir Colin left the door open to the idea. He was a charming and perceptive man. 'Let me think about it further,' he said.

More than six months later, I was asked to have lunch there again. At the entrance I stepped into the strange airlock you have to go through, feeling like something on display in a museum looking out through the glass. I was taken upstairs in the lift. Each time the lift doors opened I saw how normal everything seemed in SIS's headquarters. The offices had noticeboards with calendars and holiday postcards on them. Cups of tea and copies of newspapers were on the desks. Young men with earrings and tattoos got into the lift. Attractive women of a certain age, the Miss Moneypennys of SIS, hurried along the corridors. It could have been the headquarters of a building society. It could even have been the BBC.

I was shown into the same dining room as before, but this time the entire cast of characters had

95

changed. The old 'C' had gone, and scarcely any of his senior people were there to greet me. Now there was a new 'C', and a new group of people to meet. But there was one familiar face.

'Hello, John. Long time since Cambridge.'

A man came forward from the window, where the light had made it hard for me to see him. As we shook hands, I remembered who it was. Richard had been quite a close friend of mine when the two of us were at university in Cambridge. He was clever and serious. Like so many people from those days, I had lost touch with him. Now he was the number two man in SIS, and a few years later he became 'C' himself. The thought that I had made Nescafé at college for a future head of Britain's spies was very strange.

Lunch was nice enough, but I could see that the mood had changed completely. Sir Colin had at least been prepared to think about my idea of making a film. The new men in charge wouldn't allow it. As I left, I knew I would never be allowed to come back with a camera crew.

13. Colombia

In 1995 a TV producer I knew rang me to say that a priest she knew in Colombia, South America, had offered to take a BBC crew to film cocaine being sold to the big drug cartels, the illegal organizations that fix the prices of drugs. Was I interested? I certainly was. Colombia was the world's cocaine capital.

The priest was called Father Leonel, and he came from the little town of Remolino in southern Colombia, deep in the Amazonian forest. He promised we would be able to see the market in Remolino where the paste made from coca leaves, which would be turned into cocaine, was sold. It sounded very good. No one had ever done any filming like this before. But it was obviously going to be dangerous.

There are no roads through the

forest to Remolino. The only way to get there is by river. We would have to hire a fast boat, so we could do the entire trip in daylight. It would, we were told, be suicidal to stay anywhere along the river by night. We met up with our boatman, Raul, at dawn in the town of San Vicente, and headed off down the wide, silent, dark river. From here on we were in no-man's-land, where the gun was the only law.

This whole area of Colombia was controlled by a group of left-wing bandits known from its initials as FARC, 'the Revolutionary Armed Forces of Colombia' in English. They were heavily involved in the drugs trade. Father Leonel told us that a group of them would be in charge of the cocaine market at Remolino, and that they knew all about us. They would protect us, he said. It must have been very risky for Father Leonel, because he had to live there with all these violent people. But he wanted the world to know how bad things had become in southern Colombia.

The journey took us five hours in the hot sun. The forest was dense and beautiful on both sides of the river.

It was Saturday, and Remolino was getting ready for the next day's coca market. We walked through the little town, with everyone staring at us. Steve, the cameraman, stopped to film a butcher's stall which had the meat from a dead cow hanging up on it.

'So *that*'s what happened to the last crew to come here,' he said. We all laughed, a little too loudly. That night we slept in the priest's house beside the church.

The next morning was hot and fine. Outside, Remolino was preparing for business. The boats were arriving in large numbers, bringing buyers and sellers to market. The sellers carried plastic bags over their shoulders. These contained the thick coca paste that they were hoping to sell. It would only be turned into refined cocaine later. The buyers had leather money satchels and tough-looking bodyguards who followed them everywhere. Every market day people were ambushed and murdered here.

In spite of Father Leonel's assurances, it was a nervous time for us. Everyone except us had a gun. There was no sign of the bandits, and until they arrived the market could not start. In the narrow streets people jostled each other and looked angrily at us, but they seemed to have heard that we were here under the bandits' protection and so they didn't try to stop us filming them. Even these ferocious characters were scared of them.

It was noon before they arrived. Two of their soldiers were assigned to escort us around, and we were told we mustn't film them. In the hot, threatening little market twenty or thirty tables had been set out. Each one was equipped with sets of scales, spoons, cigarette lighters and rolls of pink toilet paper. All this kit was used for testing the coca paste, to check that it was as pure as possible.

The buyers and sellers hated the thought that we were allowed to film them. Still, the bandits' protection worked remarkably well. These were some of the most violent and dangerous people on earth, yet they did nothing more than turn their faces away from us and mutter a little. Eventually, we managed to persuade a group to buy some coca paste on camera. We had to promise not to show their faces, just their hands.

Just by being there, we had a bad effect on their business.

'What is the price today?' I asked one of the sellers, a man with a terrible scar down the side of his face. It gave his left eye a particularly sinister look.

'Fifteen hundred dollars per kilo,' he answered.

Everyone around him laughed.

'More like eight hundred and fifty dollars a kilo,' a mocking voice shouted. It was our fault, apparently. Because we were filming there, the buyers were reluctant to come forward and show their faces.

I saw that the bandit commander had arrived, together with a small group of attractive women bandits. I wanted to thank him for making sure we were safe. I went up to him and said, 'Many thanks for giving the BBC your protection.'

He turned to me and said, 'I'm not giving you anything. I don't care if you live or die.'

'Thanks a lot,' I said, and walked away.

I could see now what Father Leonel had done. He had managed to persuade the buyers and sellers that

103

the FARC were protecting us, and he had told the FARC that the buyers and sellers wanted us to be there. It had worked beautifully. I honoured him for the trick he had pulled. I also decided not to tell the others about it until we had left Remolino. Assuming, of course, that we managed to get out safely.

By now the market was coming to an end. Because of our presence, sales had been low. Even so, a million dollars had changed hands in the space of a few hours. By the time the coca supplies which had been sold here reached America and Europe, they would be worth a hundred million dollars.

It was getting dark. Raucous laughter came from the bars. In the little huts nearby, the giggling and squealing showed that the whores were hard at work. Once, I heard a loud scream. During the night three people were murdered. That made it an ordinary market day in Remolino.

We sat out in the courtyard of the priest's house, smoking cigars and drinking whisky. We were pleased with ourselves for doing an extraordinary piece of work. All the same, we were nervous. Everyone knew where we were, and the bandits were no longer around. They had gone back to their camp.

I lay on my bunk, and wondered what I would do if someone came in with a gun. I was still wondering when I fell asleep.

We were up at five the next morning, and slipped quietly through the village to the boat. Raul the boatman was waiting, and he pushed us well out into the water before turning the engine on. By that stage no one could catch us.

14. Princess Diana

Royal reporting isn't really my thing, but like most people, I was fascinated by Diana, Princess of Wales, and I thought the way the tabloids treated her was disgusting. Yet what the tabloids said in their defence was true. She did seek out publicity, and she craved attention. However the way the tabloids probed into the most intimate parts of her personal life shamed our entire society. Sometimes journalists seemed to be the only people who didn't understand this.

I first met Diana in 1989, at a state banquet at Buckingham Palace. The food and wines were superb, and at the end, by the light of several hundred candles, a lone piper circled the tables, playing in honour of the guests. Afterwards, the ordinary guests stood around in a drawing room drinking coffee. The Royal Family and the guests of honour stood in a room next to it. There was no physical barrier between the two rooms, yet no one crossed from one room to the other without being invited.

I had just come back from eastern Europe, from Romania, where I had been arrested several times. One of the royal dukes wanted to talk about all this, so I was asked to cross the magic line. Once I was in the royal room, I stayed there, chatting to other people as well. Then a voice spoke behind me.

'I've been looking forward all night to meeting you.'

I turned, and saw Diana standing there in a white dress with diamonds around her neck and in her hair. I was starstruck, of course. She knew exactly how to attract a susceptible middle-aged man like me. We talked for half an hour. Did she mind, I asked, if I didn't call her 'Your Royal

Highness'? She didn't. She told me about her life, and about the way the tabloids made her life a misery.

'If you ever need any help in that department,' I said, 'just let me know.'

I'm still not quite sure what I meant. Murder the editor of the *Sun*? Hold a royal correspondent hostage? But at that moment I'd have done anything for her.

'Thank you,' she said. 'I won't forget it.'

Then the Duchess of York came bouncing up, full of gossip. I was irritated by the interruption, but there was something quite refreshing about her informal manner. Until, that is, the Queen went past, and the Duchess of York put her tongue out behind the Queen's back. Maybe I was too easily shocked. The Duchess of York giggled and went off. Then the Prince of Wales came over, and after a few more words he and Diana walked away together.

'It was wonderful to meet you,' she said to me.

I walked all the way home, too excited to take a taxi.

On 31 August 1997 I had a call early in the morning to say that the princess had died in a car crash in Paris. That evening I wrote a story about her life for the main TV news. I tried not to be too emotional about it. Her death provided all the emotion that was needed.

Soon afterwards, it was clear that something strange was happening in British society. The Royal Family had remained at Balmoral, instead of coming to London. The two princes, William and Harry, had gone to church on the morning after the accident. It's impossible to imagine what they were feeling. We all expected the Royal Family to take the lead in the nation's mourning, but they didn't.

By Tuesday, queues were forming in the Mall. People went to pay their respects to Diana by signing a book of condolence. They were angry. They believed that the Royal Family had betrayed her. For these people she had represented the new mood of British society, softer and gentler and more democratic. The Palace still stood for the old ways. It was more strict, more in control of its emotions, even though privately the Royal Family was as shocked and sad as everyone else.

At long last, the Royal Family returned to London. The kind of things the crowds in the Mall were demanding started to happen.

The funeral the following Saturday brought everyone together. I was asked by a newspaper to write a story about it, and I was given a ticket to Westminster Abbey.

I made an early start. The morning was beautiful, with the sun shining down between the buildings. The empty streets were silent and clean. The crowds were already building up outside the Abbey. Huge TV screens had been set up in the nearby parks, so that people could watch what was happening. A queue of invited guests had formed at the gate that led to the Abbey's north door.

Once we'd got inside and sat down, there was silence. Then came a sound I shall never forget. It was the sound of soldiers' boots on the tiles of the Abbey floor. Six men carried Diana's coffin down the aisle. It still seemed impossible that so much passion and elegance could have been taken out of the world.

There had been a lot of talk that the officials at Buckingham Palace had hated Diana and had pushed her out. I was sitting beside a group of six or seven of them, all men in their fifties and sixties, perfectly dressed. Like the Royal Family, they seemed to be strongly self-controlled—the stiff-upper-lip type. As the service went on, though, I could see that more than one of them had tears running down their faces. They had obviously been as open to her charm as I was.

Earl Spencer, Diana's brother, spoke from the pulpit. His words had real power, and his mix of passion and control was just what the British people seemed to want. He was full of fury against the tabloids for hunting her down. He was also angry with the Royal Family. They had turned against her because of her private problems, but in public she was too much of a star.

I don't think I have ever heard a better speech than the one he made that day. It caught the mood of the vast crowd outside the Abbey. When it was finished there was a rustling sound, which grew louder until it swept in through the open doors of the Abbey. It was the sound of people in the parks and streets clapping. They had heard Earl Spencer on television. Inside, most of the guests also began to clap. It spread row by row, until it reached the front row where the Royal Family was sitting. They did not clap. The tradition is that you don't clap in church. The Royal Family kept to the tradition, even though no one else did.

I listened to the sound and looked at the coffin. It seemed to me that things would never be quite the same again, even for people like me who didn't know her well. Ever since that day, I have never passed Kensington Palace without thinking of the glamour that went out of London when she left.

15. Meeting Colonel Gadhafi

When I woke up I didn't know where I was. There was a strange smell, and I seemed to be trapped. Then I remembered. I was lying in a bunk on a ferry to Libya in North Africa. The smell was a mixture of fuel-oil and coffee. I rolled out of bed and joined Bob, my cameraman, for breakfast. Someone put a plate in front of me. On it was a fried egg with a dot of blood in the middle of the yolk.

'I don't really feel hungry any more,' I said to Bob.

We went up to speak to people on the deck of the ship. Most of them were gloomy about Libya's future. After the bombing of the Pan Am plane over Lockerbie in December 1988, the United Nations had asked member countries to stop trading with Libya. This had had a serious effect on the whole country. You couldn't even fly there now. That was why we were going there by boat.

'Why are you coming to Libya?' one man asked.

To interview Colonel Gadhafi, I answered. Gadhafi was Libya's leader.

'Maybe he'll tell you that he'll let those Lockerbie fellows go,' said the man.

We arrived at the port and met an official. No one looked in our bags. This was good, because I had a bottle of whisky in mine. I had forgotten that alcohol wasn't allowed in Libya. The bottle clinked when I put my suitcase down.

Then we went to a huge hotel. The beds were tiny and the carpets were filthy.

'The last time I came here to interview Gadhafi, I was stuck here for days. And he didn't give us the interview anyway,' I told Bob.

But it wasn't like last time. We were

115

told to get ready to see Gadhafi the day after next. On the day of the interview, a large black limousine came to the hotel to pick us up. We drove out of the city towards the desert.

'Where are we going?' I asked one of the men in the car.

'To see the Leader,' he said.

'Sure, but where?'

'Ah, nobody can say.'

So that was clear.

We reached a big army base. When they saw our official car, the men at the gate made a fuss about our passes and looked in the boot. We drove along a track, and as the sun began to fall we saw Gadhafi's tent. It looked just like I remembered it. It was the size of a tennis court, and covered with green, red and white canvas. Inside, the floor was covered with expensive carpets.

'Fantastic,' I said.

We weren't allowed to stop there, though. Instead, we were taken to a large camper van. We followed our guide up the steps, and found ourselves in a tiny room at the back of the van, with no windows.

'For the interview,' said our guide proudly.

'This is useless,' I said to Bob.

'Completely,' said Bob, shaking his head.

The guide looked upset. He was a nice fellow, and easily hurt.

'The only place to do it is the tent,' we said.

The tent had far more room, and was a lot more interesting as a backdrop. At last the officials all agreed, and Bob worked away in the heat, setting up his lights and testing the camera. I paced up and down, thinking of questions to ask Gadhafi. Interviews with him were always tricky.

Bob was still not ready when some officials walked over to the entrance.

'He's coming,' I warned Bob. We needed some good shots of Gadhafi walking in.

And then, through a gap in the tent, I saw him.

'Get ready, he's just coming in. You'll never guess what he looks like,' I whispered to Bob.

Gadhafi was wearing a bright shirt and an old straw hat, which he had on sideways. He was on crutches. A year before he had been in a strange accident, which some people thought might have been an attempt to kill him. Gadhafi had said he had fallen over and hurt his leg while playing football.

I expected one of the officials to ask him to take his hat off for the camera, because it made him look barking mad. But no, they just smiled and let him walk into the tent like that. He sat down and smiled, with his hat still jammed sideways on his head.

I asked him about Lockerbie. Not long before, someone from MI5 had said that the British had planned to kill him, so I asked him about that. Gadhafi gave short, vague answers, which were scarcely worth having. I was running out of questions fast. Then Gadhafi interrupted me.

'I have something to tell you. The English say two men here are guilty of the Lockerbie bombing. If they did it, there is no reason why they should not be tried for it. We think they are not guilty, but there is no reason for them to stay here. They can go to Britain.'

Suddenly I understood why we had been invited to see the Leader. He was offering up the two men to the British for trial. That would put an end to the trade ban against Libya. In the past, Gadhafi had kept the two men safe from British courts. Now he was sacrificing them. It was a scoop for Bob and me.

That evening, Bob knocked on my door.

'There's something funny about the interview,' he said.

Oh no, I thought, he means the tape's damaged.

'Nothing like that,' Bob said. 'Gadhafi was making noises, that's all.'

'What kind of noises?'

'Kind of personal ones.' He looked away.

'What, like stomach rumblings?'

'No, worse than that.'

'What, farting?'

Bob blushed and nodded.

'Look, that's stupid, Bob. If he'd been farting, I'd have heard it. You're making it up.'

'Well, listen to the tape.'

I listened. There was no doubt about it. Gadhafi would rise up a little in his seat, the thunder would roll for a few seconds, and then he would sink back looking quietly pleased with himself.

We showed the interview on the BBC News, and, although I didn't say anything about it, you could clearly hear Gadhafi breaking wind.

120

After that you could see him giving a little secret smile.

I wrote a story about it for that week's *Sunday Telegraph*. Somehow it was easier to say in a newspaper than on the BBC. Throughout our interview, I said, Colonel Gadhafi had farted long and loudly.

The paper's foreign editor was a friend of mine. He headlined my story 'Warm Wind Blows From Gadhafi'.

16. Smuggled in Disguise

No one likes journalists, and I can't say I blame them. The Taliban, who controlled most of Afghanistan, liked us least of all, especially television journalists. They used to hang television sets from lamp-posts, using videotape as rope, and whenever I went there they ordered me not to film any living creature. They said it was against the Holy Koran. When I asked them why they had allowed us to bring a television camera if there wasn't anything we could film except buildings, they just used to shrug.

But in 2001, after the attacks of 11 September and the advance on the Afghan capital, Kabul, of the Northern Alliance, who were fighting against the Taliban, they wouldn't give me a visa to enter Afghanistan at all.

There was only one thing to do—

enter the country secretly. My hope was that I might be able to smuggle myself all the way from the Pakistan border to Kabul, where I could perhaps be hidden by some resistance group. I had done this in 1989, when the Communists still controlled Kabul, and it had worked very well. Of course I would have to watch out for informers, and the penalties if I were caught could be pretty bad. But it would be an extraordinary scoop, to do a live broadcast by satellite phone right under the Taliban's noses.

So I wanted to know how far we could get inside the country. We used our contacts, and a few hours later the cameraman, Peter, found a way. A group of smugglers agreed to take us across the border and as far as we wanted to go. Their only demand was that we had to go in disguise. As women. In other words, we would have to wear burkas, the head-to-toe cloak worn by most Afghan women.

I thought it was funny. It would make a good story, and I have never been able to say no to a good story. I could see the sense in it, too. No one would be able to see who we were if we wore burkas.

We went to a market in a border town in Pakistan to buy the burkas. I explained to the shopkeeper that we wanted to take them home to our wives as presents. He was too polite to show he didn't believe us. And, when we told him we wanted to try them on ourselves, he didn't ask us why. We asked for the largest he had in stock. He hooked one down from a display near the ceiling of the shop. I put it over my head: much too small. Also, my big boots stuck out. The shopkeeper found one which looked bigger. The lace fitted directly in front of my face, as it should. I thought I looked pretty good. Directly I put it on, I seemed to vanish completely. No one even looked at me.

Outside, a small group of people had gathered. When we came out, they hooted and applauded. I bowed to them, and they loved that.

Our disguises might be silly and the whole enterprise might be dangerous, but we decided to go ahead with it. We were very careful not to talk to anyone in the hotel about our plan. We didn't even tell the BBC in London, in case they tried to stop us. The BBC isn't called 'Auntie' for nothing. It can get very protective, and it worries about you endlessly.

Peter and I set off for the Khyber Pass, the main route between Pakistan and Afghanistan, sitting side by side in the back of our vehicle. He was wearing a yellow burka, I was wearing a blue one. When we passed the army roadblocks, the soldiers peered into the car and barely gave us a glance. Our disguise was working.

We arrived that evening at a small

125

mud-brick fortress at the start of the Khyber Pass. Our driver got out to beat on the high wooden gates. At last a very old man with only one eye pulled them open to let our vehicle in. Then he slammed them shut and chained them.

We were awake at 5.30, with the cocks crowing. We had just got our kit together, and were drinking a welcome cup of tea, when there was hooting at the gate. Someone was beating on it, just like our driver had the night before. A black Toyota truck drove in, carrying four men with AK-47 rifles. They were our escort.

The smugglers didn't laugh as we put our burkas on. It had been their idea, anyway. The part which went round my head was far too tight, and I soon started getting a headache from it. The rest of the burka was excellent. It was so big and roomy that I could carry everything I wanted underneath its folds. Peter was even able to hide his camera and a bag of batteries and tapes under his.

We shook hands with our host and his servants, and climbed into the truck. We asked to sit in the truck's cab, with the driver. That meant that our four armed guards had to sit in the open at the back. We had only been going for an hour through the dust and heat when the driver stopped. He spoke to the four gunmen and then to our translator.

'He says they want you to sit in the back, out in the open,' the translator said. 'Women do not go in the front of cars here.'

We agreed, because we didn't want the gunmen to pull out of the deal.

It was a long day's drive, sitting out in the dust and the hot sun, and we got very tired. Sometimes we drove along the bed of a river, with the water coming up to the tops of the wheels. Then we went through sand dunes. The sand forced its way through the lace in our burkas and between our teeth. It was very uncomfortable, sitting out there over the rear axles. I began to realize what life was like for an Afghan woman.

Once we were in open country, Peter got out his camera and took some shaky pictures of our journey. The smugglers knew who we were and what we were there to do, but they would stay loyal to us because we had paid them. That's the law of the Khyber Pass. But it was important not to let the local people know we were there. Somebody would tell the Taliban.

Although I was supposed to be in charge, I couldn't see where we were driving. The burka made it hard for me to look around, and I couldn't even work out where the sun was. We asked the smugglers if we had crossed into Afghanistan yet. They didn't understand the question, because they had no interest in borders. We were in their area, that was all.

At last, the vehicle stopped at a farm. This was clearly a place used a lot by the smugglers. We had made it over the border. With a huge sense of pleasure and relief, we were able to take off our disguises. A crowd gathered round us, but no one laughed at the sight of two large Western men appearing from under our burkas. For a short while, I was the biggest woman in Afghanistan, with the biggest feet. And yet our disguise was so good, we weren't caught. Women count for so little in that area that none of the guards at the checkpoints even looked at us. Our burkas were like a magic cloak of invisibility.

17. A Short Walk to Kabul

The city lay below us: Kabul, at last. Standing there in the chilly November dawn, I couldn't take my eyes off it. For two months I had thought of nothing but getting back there.

I had last been in the city just before 11 September 2001—what Americans call '9/11'. On 9 September, the Taliban had ordered me out of Kabul, the capital of Afghanistan. Then the Twin Towers and the Pentagon were attacked. The Americans began organizing a way to overthrow the rulers of Afghanistan, the Taliban, who had given shelter to Osama bin Laden, the mastermind behind the bombings. The Americans had therefore given their support to the Northern Alliance, an anti-Taliban organization, and now, two months later, the Northern Alliance had advanced on Kabul and was at the city gates. And I was with them.

The Northern Alliance had orders not to enter Kabul, for fear of causing a bloodbath. My BBC team and I naturally wanted to get into the city. To do so we would have to ignore the Northern Alliance's orders and head into Kabul on our own. Would my BBC team come with me? After living with them for so many weeks, I felt sure they would, though it might be very risky. The Taliban and al-Qaeda were still thought to be in control of the city.

A tough-looking soldier from the Northern Alliance stood in the road. His back was to Kabul, his face towards us. He had orders not to let anyone pass. And yet he wasn't the main barrier. That was the man in charge of the advance on Kabul, General Haidar. He had smashed through the Taliban front line. Now he would have to agree to let us go in. After that, we would have to see if the Taliban fired on us as we entered the city.

We were the only journalists around at this key moment. If we were stopped here now, it could be a long time before we got down to Kabul. The rest of the world's journalists, who were several hours behind us, would have a chance of catching up. We couldn't have that. Peter, the cameraman, asked General Haidar if we could go to Kabul.

'He says the road is too dangerous,' Peter said to me.

'But will he stop us if we go on foot?'

Peter asked him.

'Well, if you're going to go on foot . . .' said the General. He was a good friend of Peter's, and he was too embarrassed to refuse. He ordered a soldier to go with us, to give us a bit of protection.

I set off down the hill, hoping that the others would follow me. They were a wonderful bunch. My other cameraman, Joe, had broken a bone in his foot a few days earlier. But, when I told him I wouldn't let him come with me into Kabul, he insisted that he wouldn't stay behind. We got someone to try and sort his foot out for him, and I fed him the big painkillers my doctor had given me in case of serious injury. So, in spite of his broken foot, Joe was hobbling along with us. It made me very proud of the people I was with.

The first part of the road was pretty steep, and we went down it fast. The others weren't just going to let me go first and follow my lead. It was turning into a kind of race!

The closer we got to the city, the bigger the crowds became. I could hear people shouting 'BBC London'. The word was already getting round about who we were. Huge numbers of Afghans listened to the BBC's broadcasts in their own languages, and the BBC was very popular. They knew that the Northern Alliance must be close behind us, and that they had been freed from Taliban rule.

People reached out to grab me and shake my hand. After the weeks of waiting and anxiety and outright fear, I felt full of joy. I raised my arms to greet the crowds, forcing my way through them. A bus was stuck in the crowd, and everyone inside it tried to touch me through the windows. I grabbed as many hands as I could, laughing with the relief and pleasure of it all. To be the first journalists to enter the most closed and difficult city on earth was a superb moment.

Ahead, I could see the sign in the middle of the road which marked the entrance to Kabul. One of our team was a little ahead of me, as he had been for much of our walk. I sped up, wanting to be the first to pass the sign. This was childish, of course. After all, what did it matter which of us got past it first? But I was still in the grip of the will to win. That desire had brought us all here in the first place, far ahead of our rivals.

My legs were hurting from walking downhill so fast. I looked at my watch: 7.53 a.m. Kabul was no longer a Taliban city, and no one had fired a shot at us.

By now the crowds were huge. I had been so caught up in the thrill of the moment that I hadn't thought to look back at the others, and anyway there was no chance of our sticking together with so many people pushing and shoving us. Now, when I checked, I realized that most of them had vanished. I found out later that Peter, the cameraman, had fallen over and damaged his camera lens. Joe had had to stop because the pain in his foot was too great. He managed to get a taxi to our meeting point, the Intercontinental Hotel. Two of the others had borrowed bicycles—crowds in a revolution are always remarkably generous and helpful, I've found. There were only two others still with me: the Afghan soldier, and a wonderful American translator called John Jennings. I decided that we needed transport. I spotted a taxi creeping through the crowd, and the three of us got into it. 'Hotel Intercontinental,' I said to the driver grandly. Actually he was the one who did best out of it, since the fare was five American dollars and I only had a hundred-dollar note. He got a ninety-five dollar tip!

I thought I would be the first into the hotel, but, as I was checking in, two of the others came forward out of the darkness, laughing. They were the ones who had come by bicycle, and they were still laughing at having beaten me to it. The rest arrived safely soon afterwards.

I sat in the sunshine on the roof of the hotel, waiting to go live on BBC Radio 4. I felt so proud to have been part of this group of ours. We were hours and hours ahead of the entire world's press into Kabul after two months of the hardest living and travelling I had ever experienced. It was an amazing scoop. And I still felt thrilled by the welcome the crowds in the street had given us. I suppose that's why I wasn't a little more careful in what I said on air.

Down the line I heard the voice of Sue McGregor, the Radio 4 presenter. 'I don't understand,' she said. 'If the Northern Alliance troops didn't enter the city, but the Taliban have gone, who freed Kabul?'

Sitting there in the sunshine, enjoying the pleasure of it all, I made a mistake. Quite a bad one, as it turned out. I made a joke.

'I suppose it was the BBC,' I said.

The British press, which doesn't like the BBC much, never let me forget it, and I still get teased about it to this day. But I didn't mind. It had been a wonderful, unforgettable experience.

18. The Capture of Saddam

Sometimes we are betrayed by those who are closest to us.

Mohammed al-Musslit was the best of Saddam's bodyguards, the most loyal and the most tough. He guarded his leader during the last days of fighting before Baghdad fell on 9 April 2003, and they escaped together as the Americans secured the city .

He stayed with Saddam during many of his eight months of wanderings, and he knew most of the hiding places that had been prepared in case Saddam should need them. It was said that the men who created these hiding places were all killed to make sure they didn't talk.

The Americans found al-Musslit through good, old-fashioned police work. They traced all the people they could find who might know where

Saddam was, and in the end they tracked al-Musslit down. He was a strong man, and a tough one. His nickname was 'the fat one', but he wasn't at all soft. He stood up to being questioned for a long time, but eventually he broke.

Although the Americans used torture on some of their prisoners, they don't seem to have tortured him. In fact torture is usually pointless. It is more a way of letting the captors express their rage and hatred than a good way to get information. Eventually a prisoner who is being tortured will make up any story to please his questioners and make the pain stop. So what he tells you has no real value. On the other hand, people say that the strongest person will break through lack of sleep and clever questioning. It's still a kind of torture, but it doesn't involve pain.

On Sunday 15 December, al-Musslit finally gave in and told them where Saddam was hiding. The Americans flew him to the town of Tikrit, the place which had always been Saddam's power base. There they made him point out the two places nearby where Saddam had hidden in the past. Then they called in six hundred troops to examine the sites. It was six o'clock in the evening when the soldiers arrived, and already dark. For two and a half hours they searched the two areas with bright lamps and torches, but they found nothing.

One of the places they examined was a small compound close to the River Tigris, nothing more than a couple of lonely huts. They had searched there before, and found nothing. This time, though, one thing was different. Even though the place seemed entirely deserted, an old orange and white taxi was parked nearby, the kind you see all over Iraq. Two local men were sitting in it. They seemed stupid and scared, and couldn't answer questions.

There was an area in the compound with two beds, a few clothes and basic items for washing. Next door was an open kitchen and a toilet. I visited the place myself three days later. It would never have occurred to me that Saddam Hussein might be hiding out there.

Outside the huts there was a lot of rubbish on the ground, and a bit of carpet was lying there. The soldiers were starting to give up the search, but one of them bent down and looked closely at this bit of carpet. He suddenly had the feeling that it hadn't been been thrown away—that it might have been put there on purpose. The soldier picked it up. Underneath was a square bit of board smeared with mud. He picked up the board too, and as it came away it revealed a hole in the ground.

It came as a total surprise. Another soldier pulled out a hand-grenade and was about to throw it down the hole. The others stopped him. They shone torches down the hole. Two hands appeared in the light of the torches. Whoever was in the hole was going to surrender. Then they saw a head, with a dirty beard.

'My name is Saddam Hussein,' said the head, in English. 'I am the president of Iraq, and I want to make a deal.' He had been on the run for 250 days.

'Regards from President Bush,' said one of the soldiers, and the others laughed.

Saddam had a pistol with him in the hole, but when he stood up to surrender he left it lying by his feet. He had decided not to resist. It was just like him to think he could still make a deal at a time like that. Maybe later he realized it would have been better for his reputation if he had died fighting. That might have united Muslims across the world. Instead, a lot of people had contempt for him.

The hole was 2.4 metres at its deepest. Saddam was a heavy man in his sixties, and he couldn't have climbed out of it without help. If the men who had been guarding him had left or been arrested, Saddam might well have starved to death.

There were no radios or mobile phones at the compound. Saddam and his men knew that the Americans would be listening for any sign of him. If he had made any calls, they would have been able to trace him straight away. The soldiers found $750,000 in cash, two rifles and a case full of important papers.

It was hard for his supporters to accept that he had given up so easily. Journalists in many Arab newspapers suggested that Saddam must have been drugged. Some said that his capture must have taken place weeks or months earlier. In the television coverage of the hiding place you could see a date tree, which was growing near the hole in the ground, and many people insisted that the dates on it were old, and that therefore the pictures of the arrest must have been shot long before. But I looked at the dates carefully when I went there. They were perfectly young.

Saddam's favourite daughter, Raghad, was interviewed in Jordan. She agreed that he must have been drugged. He would never have surrendered otherwise, she said. 'A lion is still a lion, even when it has been caught.'

But after the first shock of his capture, no one seemed to regard him as a lion any more. Saddam had asked other people to pay the highest price, and yet at the crucial moment he had not been willing to pay it himself. Instead, he had simply surrendered. Even two of Saddam's hated sons had died fighting the Americans. Saddam had been a fighter all his life; even his name,

Saddam, meant 'the one who confronts'. Now, it seemed, he had lost everything.

By betraying his leader, Mohammed al-Musslit lost everything too: his honour, his self-respect and his reputation. For the rest of his life he would be in danger from anyone who wanted to kill him. He couldn't even claim the huge reward offered by the Americans to the person who led them to Saddam, because he didn't come to them and tell them voluntarily. Mohammed al-Musslit's life was destroyed. Like his boss, he was a dead man who had kept on living.

19. Disaster in Iraq

There were seven of us in the BBC team covering the second Gulf War in northern Iraq in 2003. Tom was directing a film about our war. Oggy was the producer. Dragan was a friend of mine from Belgrade, in Serbia, who fixed things and did some of the filming. Fred was the cameraman. Craig was our security adviser. Kamaran, who came from the town where we were based, was our translator. He was a charming young man.

One morning in April, the Iraqi army began to crack. The Kurdish people, who had been oppressed by Saddam Hussein for years, but who had, in 1991, won some control of the part of Iraq in which they lived, were keen to see the back of Saddam once and for all. Their forces, backed up by the Americans,

146

advanced into territory which Saddam's men had been holding. We drove up to the front line, and decided to head for a nearby town which the Kurds had just captured.

Being out in no-man's-land like this felt very dangerous. The Iraqis were firing their guns in our direction. And they weren't the only source of danger. After covering several wars which the Americans have been involved in, I knew that they have a long tradition of killing people on their own side by mistake. 'Friendly fire', it's called; not a very clever name.

The whole area was ominously empty. There were explosions close by, but it was hard to know exactly what was causing them. I decided that we should stop by the side of the road. Everyone agreed. At that moment there was a roar of engines behind us in the distance. It was a convoy of American and Kurdish special forces.

'It's Waji,' said Kamaran. Waji was a very senior Kurdish soldier, and this was an important convoy. They caught up with us. If we stay with them, I argued to myself, we will be safe. The Iraqis wouldn't know who they were, and the Americans obviously won't attack their own side. Or so I thought.

Ahead of us lay a ridge, and the vehicles stopped there. Two Iraqi tanks were firing in our direction, but the shells were landing some way behind us. A couple of American planes were circling the battlefield at around a thousand feet. Close enough, I was sure, to see the huge stars and stripes flags that the American vehicles were flying. Close enough to see that most of the vehicles in the convoy were American Humvees. Close enough to see the large panels of orange material that covered the roof of every vehicle, including ours. That was the sign the Western forces all

148

displayed, and we had copied them for safety.

'Flak-jacket time,' I said, even so.

Waji and his men were standing on the ridge looking down towards the Iraqi tanks in the valley below. As they watched, one of them fired a shell in our general direction. An American officer got on the radio, calling in an air strike on the tank.

The two American planes were flying lower than ever now, checking out the whole battlefield. Fred wanted to film them, and he asked Tom and Craig to get his tripod from the car.

Then disaster struck.

There was a huge explosion. I was only twelve yards away from the bomb as it landed right in the middle of the group of American and Kurdish soldiers. I actually saw it as it left the aircraft, and then as it hit the ground—a flash of silver and red. The only reason I and my colleagues survived is that we were standing to the side of it. The full blast destroyed the entire area immediately in front of the bomb.

All the same, I was hit by fourteen pieces of shrapnel. Most of them were small, but at least two were big enough to have killed me, if they had hit my face or chest. My left eardrum was blasted away, and one piece of shrapnel, as large as a nine-millimetre bullet, hit me near the hip and knocked me down. Some of my clothes were ripped off by the explosion.

I was unconscious for a second or two. Then I felt myself being pulled up. Instead of running for shelter, Dragan had come back to help me. He thought the plane might drop a second bomb.

Ahead of us, Fred was kneeling down. His face and glasses were covered in thick blood. It was a shocking sight.

'Is my eye OK?' he kept asking. Dragan told him it was fine, in order to calm him down. Neither of us thought it could be.

The two planes were still flying overhead.

'Call your bloody friends off,' I shouted at the Americans on the ground.

By now most of the Kurdish trucks from the convoy were on fire. Many of them were carrying rockets or grenades, which began exploding. One flew just inches over our heads.

I went to see what had happened to the others. I heard terrible screams. A man passed by me holding his insides in his arms. He seemed quite calm, and was looking around for a place to sit down. Half a minute later, he was dead. Another man was burning to death right in front of me. There was nothing I could do to save him. The smell made me gag, and I stumbled away. More and more bodies were burning alive as I looked.

Most of the area was covered with

151

flames and thick smoke. Tom and Craig were in there somewhere.

At that moment Craig came staggering through the smoke. 'Where's Kamaran?' he was saying.

'No idea,' I shouted. 'Is Tom OK?'

Then I saw him too. Later Tom told me how he had survived. Just before the bomb dropped he was walking towards a group of Kurdish soldiers to speak to them. Every one of those soldiers would die within seconds. But at that precise moment Tom's satellite phone rang. It was his mother, wishing him a happy birthday.

He turned round to get a better signal, and walked away from the group of soldiers again. Then the bomb fell. For minutes on end Tom staggered through the flames and smoke, trying to recover and get to safety. He had a piece of shrapnel in his foot, but was otherwise unharmed. Finally he glanced down at the phone, and realized his mother had heard the whole thing.

'Mum, Mum, I'm all right,' he said.

'Yes, I know, darling,' said his mother in her calm way. 'I could hear the language you were using.'

I dialled the BBC in London. There was quite a wait before I got through. Bullets and grenades were still exploding around me. I'm going to die here, I thought, while I hang on, waiting to speak to someone. Soon, though, a studio presenter was asking me questions: the right questions.

'It was an American plane that dropped the bomb right beside us,' I said. 'I saw it land about twelve yards away, I think. This is just a scene from hell here. All the vehicles are on fire. There are bits of bodies on the ground. This is a really bad own goal by the Americans.'

They had found Kamaran by now. He had been standing close beside me, but had been hit by a big piece of shrapnel which had cut off one of his feet and injured the other. He was losing a lot of blood.

He called out for Tom. Tom knelt beside him and held him, and told him he would be OK, but he could see that Kamaran wouldn't last much longer. I could see it too.

I couldn't bear to watch any more. I had led Kamaran into this. He had only joined us as our translator, because he said he had seen my reporting and liked me, and because he wanted a bit of excitement. I might not have killed Kamaran, but he was only with us because of me.

As I walked away I saw the American soldier who had called for the air strike. His face was terrible to see. Had he given the plane the wrong position to bomb? Or had the pilot and navigator made the mistake? The Americans never held any real inquiry. There was no investigation, and there were no charges. Eighteen people had died horrible deaths, forty-eight people had been wounded, and yet the American military never seemed to want to know what had really happened.

'In war,' a senior American officer told me, 'mistakes happen.'

'There might be fewer mistakes if someone was occasionally held responsible,' I replied.

Yet I wasn't really angry for myself, or for my close colleagues. I lost the hearing of my ear, and the shrapnel in my hip will give me pain for the rest of my life. But it seems wrong to complain, given that we had had the most amazing escape any of us had ever heard of.

Not Kamaran, though. He died of his injuries within minutes, a healthy, happy, intelligent, good-looking young man of twenty-five, with everything to live for. His family adored him, and they depended on the money he earned. There had been no escape for him, no wonderful stroke of good luck. He had died a nasty, painful, frightening death, lying on the open back of a truck bouncing over an appalling road, the life-blood pumping out of him.

That afternoon, with Kamaran's blood still on me, I went to see Kamaran's mother. She was still bemused, rather than angry.

'He told me he never went to the front line. Why was he there?' she said.

He hadn't told her what he was doing, because he didn't want her to worry.

Then she said, 'The Americans know everything. How could they not know they were bombing you?'

I sat there, unable to answer her. Looking at her tragic, lined face, watching her trying to come to terms with the thought that her wonderful son, whose pictures were hanging all round the room, would never be coming back again, I had no words of comfort to give. What could I say?

That the rest of us had had a lucky escape? She couldn't have cared if everyone else had died, just as long as she could keep her son alive. Could I say that it was a worthwhile sacrifice? That his death had helped someone else? That the world would be a better place as a result? Her world was utterly destroyed, and to her nothing would ever matter so much again. Her daughter ushered me out. None of the family seemed to blame me; they just couldn't understand why it had all happened.

I had to go back and edit our report. No one who saw them would forget the dreadful pictures, or the big drop of blood that fell from the cameraman's forehead and splashed over the lens. I tried to keep my report calm and factual, and not get emotional about it. The facts were, after all, dreadful enough. I wasn't even angry with the American forces: it was American medics who tried to save Kamaran's life, and who helped us. It was just a stupid, pointless, horribly destructive mistake, that was all.

That night I slept deeply, without dreaming. In the morning I turned on the TV and saw that BBC World was still showing our report. I saw the immediate aftermath of the bomb, the splash of blood on the lens, the man whose guts had fallen out, the burned bodies. And I saw Kamaran being lifted on to the truck, a few minutes before he died. The tears ran down my face. I found myself saying the same thing, again and again and again.

'I'm so sorry. I'm so very, very sorry.'

20. Nelson Mandela

I've seen a lot of wars and violence in my career. I've watched people being tortured, without being able to do anything to help them. I've seen people injured and killed in front of my eyes: Kamaran, in Iraq, for instance. Yet I have also seen wonderful, unexpected things—forgiveness and kindness and love defeating hatred and bitterness. To end with, let me give you an example of the better side of my job.

A friend of mine, Mark Billinge, is a senior figure at the college at Cambridge University where, back in the distant 1960s, I was a student. Some years ago, he and other people at Magdalene College had a daring idea. The college had strong links with South Africa, and they decided to honour Nelson Mandela with a special degree.

When Mark told me, though, I didn't believe it would happen. Mandela was getting frail, for one thing. On his previous visit to Britain, people from all the universities that wanted to give him honours had to go to London, and do it in a single ceremony, so as not to tire him out. The idea that he would go all the way to Cambridge to visit one small college seemed highly unlikely.

Then, at the start of 2000, I started getting messages from Mark that it really was going to happen. The college offered to let me cover the event for the BBC, and I grabbed the chance. On 1 May, I arrived with my wife Dee (who is South African, and often works as my television producer) to get ready for the big event the next day.

It must sound like a very easy story to cover. Everything was laid on for us, and there was no question of having to struggle or take risks. And no competition, either. We had the story to ourselves, since the college wanted it that way.

And yet there was one very real difficulty. The South African officials in London said they didn't want me to interview Mandela. There were political problems in South Africa, and they were worried that Mandela might say something critical of the man who had taken over from him as president. But I knew we had to have an interview with him. Our report would look very strange without it. Anyway, I had promised the BBC I would speak to him, and I didn't like to let them down.

I explained all this to Mark, who promised to do what he could to help me. I also had a good team. I was still nervous, though.

On the morning of the big day, we all gathered in a café across the river from the college and made our plans. Then we moved into the garden at the back of the college, where Mandela's helicopter was due to land.

I looked around the lovely lawn. When I was a student, I had danced till four in the morning and partied here. That was just when Nelson Mandela was starting his long jail sentence, which lasted twenty-seven years. At the time I was too young, and too happy, and too unaware of the outside world, to spare him a thought. And too selfish, I suppose.

But then, a decade later, in 1976, I became the BBC correspondent in South Africa during the darkest period of apartheid, the cruel system they had there which meant that the blacks and whites were kept separate by law. For instance, there were notices on the park benches to tell black people they couldn't sit there, and anyone who protested against the system could be beaten up, jailed or even killed.

Ten years after that, I returned to South Africa to watch as apartheid started to crumble. I was there in 1990 when Nelson Mandela walked out of prison a free man. I was there when he became president after an election which almost everyone had forecast would be a bloodbath. And I was there when the election turned into a wonderful, inspiring occasion instead, because of Mandela's willingness to forgive his enemies.

There was the faint sound of a helicopter in the clouds above us. It settled down on the grass of the college garden, and the door opened. Slowly, Nelson Mandela stepped out. People moved forward to shake hands and welcome him. He was grinning his infectious smile the whole time.

My wife Dee and her sister Gina (whom we had smuggled in) came forward to shake his hand. He spoke to them in their own language,

Afrikaans, which had once been the language of apartheid but which he had encouraged and supported as president. I knew from my own experience how good he made you feel when he spoke to you. Helped by his aides, Mandela walked towards the college buildings. He stopped and joked with the people who had gathered there, waiting to see him. You could see their faces light up, as Dee's and Gina's had. The smiles stayed on their faces for a long time afterwards.

After a brief ceremony in the college chapel, Mandela was brought into a grand room nearby. It was here that we were waiting. Mark Billinge had organized things cleverly, so that I could ask Mandela some questions. Mandela always enjoyed speaking on camera, and he was perfectly happy to do it now. But his press minder, a tough blonde woman, started to get angry. She urged the South African High

Commissioner, who was also a woman, to move in and stop me. The High Commissioner tugged at my jacket the whole time I was interviewing him, trying to make me keep quiet, but I took no notice. These officials get too big for their boots sometimes.

After we'd got our interview, I felt a lot more relaxed. Which was good, since the climax of the ceremony was about to take place in the college hall.

In this hall, two centuries earlier, the master of the college had spoken out against slavery and had promised to do what he could to get it stopped. It was the place where, in October 1963, I had first met my fellow students, and many of the friends I made here at that time are still friends of mine today. Now, at the age of fifty-six, I was back here in the presence of this amazing man.

It seemed to me that, although I had never realized it, Mandela and

165

everything he stood for had been an important part of my entire life. And this occasion was to be the high point of it all.

Mandela stood up and began to speak. He felt rather nervous about being here, he said.

'This is for three reasons. Firstly, I am an old-age pensioner.'

There was a quiet little buzz of amusement from the audience.

'Secondly, I am unemployed.'

The laughter was louder this time.

'And thirdly, I have a very *baaaaad* criminal record.'

A huge wave of laughter and applause followed that.

The end of the ceremony was the most magical part of all. Up in the gallery, above our heads, the choir began singing a beautiful African song. Mandela got slowly to his feet, smiling and moving in time to the music.

One by one, the professors of the college also stood up in their brilliant scarlet, gold and purple gowns. They began dancing to the music too—some embarrassed and ill at ease, others not self-conscious at all. You could almost hear the joints creaking. As for me, I was so full of happiness and pleasure that I could hardly speak.

But I had to. The one thing that was missing from our report was a piece to camera, and I had to do it while everyone was still in the hall. I pulled myself together as best I could, straightened my tie, and looked into the camera lens.

'This college has been in existence for 573 years,' I said, 'but it's never seen anything like this.'

It really hadn't. An African leader, who had endured the worst treatment imaginable and had emerged from it to forgive his enemies and govern them in love and peace, had come to my own small Cambridge college and danced for joy with us all.

I promise you, all the bad and cruel and unhappy things I had seen in my life just seemed to fade away when I saw that.